PRAYER THE GREAT JOURNEY

DISCOVERING THE UNLIMITED POTENTIAL AND JOY OF PRAYER

ROBBY ATWOOD

FOREWORD BY **JUSTIN RIZZO**

PRAYER: THE GREAT JOURNEY
Discovering the Unlimited Potential and Joy of Prayer

Copyright © 2016 by Robby Atwood
All rights reserved. This book or any portion thereof
may not be reproduced or used in any manner whatsoever
without the express written permission of the publisher
except for the use of brief quotations in a book review.

Printed in the United States of America

ISBN 978-1-6286305-6-5

Scripture quotations taken from the following sources:

The ESV® Bible (The Holy Bible, English Standard Version®) copyright 2001 by Crossway, a publishing ministry of Good News Publishers. ESV® Text Edition: 2011. The ESV® text has been reproduced in cooperation with and by permission Good News Publishers. Unauthorized reproduction of this publication is prohibited. All rights reserved.

Scripture quotations taken from the New American Standard Bible®, Copyright © 1960, 1962, 1963, 1968, 1971, 1972, 1973, 1975, 1977, 1995 by The Lockman Foundation Used by permission. (www.Lockman.org)

Scripture quotations marked (NLT) are taken from the Holy Bible, New Living Translation, copyright © 1996, 2004, 2007, by Tyndale House Foundation. Used by permission of Tyndale House Publishers, Inc., Carol Stream, Illinois 60188. All rights reserved.

Scripture taken from the New King James Version® (NKJV). Copyright © 1982 by Thomas Nelson, Inc. Used by permission. All rights reserved

The Holy Bible, New International Version®, NIV® Copyright © 1973, 1978, 1984, 2011 by Biblica,Inc.® Used by permission. All rights reserved worldwide.

94 Southport Dr.
Somerset, KY 42501

www.one27publishing.com

DEDICATION

I dedicate this book to my best friend and amazing wife, Misty. Time and time again she has listened to me as I shared my dreams and has been such an encouragment along the way. I know that my words and dreams will always be welcome in her company. Being such an intricate part of this book, I couldn't imagine a better person to dedicate it to. Not only is she the most amazing wife, she is also a tremendous mother. The way she cares for and loves our children is truly out of this world.

Misty, I love you!

TABLE OF CONTENTS

	Foreward	1
one	Introduction	5
two	My Own Story	31
three	Praying from Identity	45
four	The Secret Place	61
five	Kings & Priests	85
six	Bold Before the Throne	117
seven	Praying in the Spirit	131
eight	My House Shall Be Called	153
nine	Practicality of Prayer	165
	A Letter from the Author	186

FOREWORD
by Justin Rizzo

Growing up as a pastor's kid in upstate New York, I attended a lot of meetings at church. I enjoyed worship meetings and teaching meetings and I especially liked those weeklong revival meetings when the visiting preacher would pray for people at the end. But probably the hardest meetings of all for me to attend were prayer meetings. I mostly viewed prayer as a religious duty that I was trying to perform to get in God's good graces and somehow find His approval. Prayer felt like a mold that I was constantly trying to fit myself into and it seemed like I could never quite make it. I grew up feeling like a failure at prayer. I have found this to be true for many people I've talked to about the subject. But God is beginning to change that.

One of the best expressions I've heard about prayer is this: "Turn your thoughts into prayer." Simply put, prayer is talking to God. It was never meant to be seen as a religious duty or a task we only do when we need something from God. Prayer is the primary way we commune with God. This is how He set up His Kingdom.

There is no specific way in which we have to pray. There is no specific room in which we have to pray. The enemy would seek to try to convince us that we have to wait to walk into "Sunday" morning church or a prayer room to pray, but God desires that we make prayer a part of our lifestyle every day, no matter where we are or what we are doing.

We are all consumed with many things. The cares of this life and weights of the world are seeking to take the love, hope, and joy away from us. We were meant to experience God. He longs to be known by His creation. Jesus said, "This is eternal life, that they would know You, the only true God, and Jesus Christ, whom you have sent" (Jn. 17:3). These are some of the last words of Jesus before He walked the Calvary road to suffer and die and as such, they are words that every person is called to live by.

God so loved the world that He gave His Son. Jesus gave His life as a ransom for our sins. But the story doesn't stop there. We were never meant to simply be forgiven and then walk through life alone. We were meant to commune with God. Prayer is the way we commune with Him and in that communion, we find true life.

Prayer is a vast subject to discuss and unpack. Many books have been penned on the topic by some amazing heroes of the faith throughout history. Each and every one of them brings unique perspective and insight that can bless the body of Christ. *Prayer: The Great Journey* continues this rich tradition by challenging and encouraging its readers into a life of deeper dependence on God.

Forward

I have personally known Robby Atwood for many years and have seen firsthand that he is a man who doesn't just preach or talk about prayer; he prays. He doesn't just speak a message; he lives that message. Robby's book doesn't just provide information. It shares practical application with such simplicity and excellence that the message can change your everyday life." Prayer - The Great Journey" will lead you down a pathway of communion and into the heart of the uncreated God who is longing to encounter you.

JUSTIN RIZZO

– Intercessory Missionary IHOP-KC

one
Introduction

You're holding in your hands a work that has been going on in my life and that is still going on inside my heart. This is a book on my journey as well as the truths that I've encountered along the way. When trying to decide on what I wanted to "debut" into the vast realm of book writing, I didn't have to think twice - not because I'm a professional on the topic. I knew instantly because, along with the knowledge of God, it has been the most impactful thing to my journey and walk with Jesus. Releasing great joy and guarding me from much sorrow, it has had more impact on my heart than the kindest words from the greatest friend. So, I have decided to write on prayer!

> *"I have been driven many times upon my knees by the overwhelming conviction that I had no where else to go. My own wisdom and that of all about me seemed insufficient for that day."*
>
> – Abraham Lincoln

Prayer was once among many things that I tried. Now, prayer is many times the first thing I do in a situation. It was once just a garment among many, now it's the thread that I intertwine in most of life's activities. This has little to do with my own personal zeal and discipline, and much to do with the fact that I am fully convinced that He longs to hear and help me in my journey. He loves to draw near to those who draw near to Him. I'll say this up front, I don't pray because I'm some "Super-Christian," I pray because I realize I need His leadership front and center in my life. Many times, prayer is our only hope!

> *Prayer must be our first retreat, never our last resort.*

Scripture makes it clear that prayer is not for the ones who have it all figured out, or the ones that have all the right answers to life's questions… Rather, prayer is for the exact opposite - the ones who are needy and frail. It's for those who have seen their own limitations, and who are learning to lean. Like Mother Theresa once said, "Prayer is putting oneself in the hands of God, at His disposition, and listening to His voice in the depth of our hearts."

> *"As for me, I am poor and needy, but the Lord takes thought for me. You are my help and my deliverer; do not delay, O my God!"*
>
> — Psalm 40:17 (ESV)

This book is about my journey in prayer. It's a result of lessons learned, both pitfalls and successes, as well as the many breakthroughs in the place of prayer. You'll hear some interesting accounts of my own prayer life, as well as the revelations I've encountered in it. Over time, these lessons and revelations have only stirred my heart to go deeper in my walk with Jesus. Each "glory to glory" encounter has shaped my life. My hope is that He uses this book to encourage you to go deeper in the Lord, and to lay aside all weight for the great purpose of seeking Him wholeheartedly. There is no greater success in life than receiving and walking in His love.

DEFINING PRAYER

Prayer. Much can be said about the subject. For in prayer lies the ability to commune with God, grow in our faith, loose chains, destroy yokes, strengthen our identity, release healing, speak blessing, and so much more. Prayer is simple yet profound. It's a subject that can be easily explained yet thoroughly expounded upon. From the art of intercession to the glories of praying in the Spirit, the subject of prayer can be an extensive one.

In the King James translation, there are over 500 passages that speak of prayer. The words "pray, prayed, prayer, prayers, prayest, prayeth, praying" occur 545 times. This doesn't include "cry out, intercede, petition, beseech" or any other terms related to prayer. The Bible is a book of prayers. In the Greek language, "pray" is proseuchomai meaning "to ask, supplicate, worship to God." Root words include pros meaning "forward, toward, the side of, near to." In the Hebrew, pray is tephillah meaning "intercession, entreaty, supplication."

When you merge these various meanings together, you get "to ask, petition, supplicate and worship toward and near to God." Petition is asking on behalf of someone, whereas supplication is

> *Prayer is the act of aiming the arrowhead of our affections and desires towards God.*

asking on behalf of yourself. In plain sense, prayer is interaction with heaven. It's conversation with God. Expressed many different ways, it's simply talking and communicating with God.

We clearly see that worship is at the heart of prayer. Just as there are (at least) 7 Hebrew words for praise, there are also many angles and approaches to prayer. In fact, prayer and praise (worship) are closely related, and actually function on the same plane. The Hebrew word for Psalms is tehillim meaning "songs of praise." "Book of Psalms" is the Hebrew word sepher tehillim meaning "book of praise." Yet, we can clearly see that Psalms is also a book of prayers, petitions, and supplications to God. Strong's points this out saying, "in the sense of prayer, it stands also in the titles of Psalms 17, 86, 90, 102, 142…" In fact, both prayer (tephillah) and praise (tehillim) derive from the same root word. They are one and the same. One of the Hebrew words for praise is tehillah meaning "new song," and denotes a spontaneous and inspired song (prayer). Therefore, praise is simply "melodic prayers." It's musical conversation.

When we adore the Lord in song, we are adding tones and melodies to our prayers and desires. For many reasons, God designed us to make melody and to sing our prayers. Can you think of a song you've learned that is purely scripture? Think of the worship song from the 1980's, "As the Deer." It's based on Psalm 42. Many in the Charismatic movement grew up singing this song and I'm sure some of you can sing it right now on the spot. You may not be able to quote the Psalm back to me, but I'm sure you can sing it. That's because God designed music and prayer to go together. It's much easier to memorize in song than in our talking voice isn't it! What about many of the hymns which are composed of hundreds of words, could you imagine trying to memorize those in your head apart from melody? Of course not. Yet, when we add melody and music to the words, many of us can recite the song with little to no effort.

> *"...speaking to one another in psalms and hymns and spiritual songs, singing and making melody with your heart to the Lord; always giving thanks for all things in the name of our Lord Jesus Christ to God, even the Father..."*
>
> *– Ephesians 5:19 (NASB)*

Heaven's throne (governmental center) runs day and night, with prayer and worship mingled together. Revelation 5:8 tells us that the living creatures and elders hold bowls (signifying prayers of the saints) and harps (signifying the worship music). This combination of worship music and intercessory prayer unites heaven into one song and prayer. Music just has that ability.

PRAYER, THE PRIMARY TOOL

Everyone in life is building something. We were made to build, because that's what God does - He loves to build things. The writer of Hebrews calls Him the great "master builder" (Hebrews 3:4). As the great architect with the master blueprint, He calls us to labor with Him. Many are building their fame or reputation, some their bank accounts, while others may be building their ministry or legacy. Whatever it may be, the point is we are all building something. This is what we were made to do. In fact, with the intent of "reaching God," we see that it didn't take long for man to start building massive structures (Genesis 11). We were made to build.

Jesus describes building this way:

> "Therefore everyone who hears these words of Mine and acts on them, may be compared to a wise man who **built his house** on the rock. And the rain fell, and the floods came, and the winds blew and slammed against that house; and yet it did not fall, for it had been founded on the rock. Everyone who hears these words of Mine and does not act on them, will be like a foolish man who **built his house** on the sand. The rain fell, and the floods came, and the winds blew and slammed against that house; and it fell—and great was its fall."
>
> — Matthew 7:24-27 (NASB)

This passage teaches several principles in building our lives with wisdom and longevity. I think it's interesting that the first condition of building a lasting house is "to hear." Jesus, the Master Builder, says "everyone who hears these words of Mine…" Although I agree with the traditional teaching of building our life around the word (rock), there is something here that we need to further inventory - it's the realm of hearing. (I know you may be saying, "what about the 'acts on them' part?") I totally acknowledge this truth and that works should be mingled with hearing, but for the sake of time, I won't dive into that right now. I want to focus on the hearing part.

Anyway, Jesus says "everyone who hears…" The Greek word for hear is "to attend to, consider what is or has been said." I especially love the meaning, "to perceive by the ear what is announced in one's presence." So, we have Jesus teaching us to attend to, consider, and to stand in one's presence that we may perceive His voice. This is how He instructs us to build. He wants a foundation of hearing. He doesn't say, "pick up a hammer and start working." Rather, He says, "slow down and hear my voice." Just sit in My presence and be! The hearing must come before the doing. He made us human BEings, not human doings. It's even interesting that God's name (Yahweh, we say Jehovah) means "to be." So according to the Son of Man, those who have a hearing ear are those who will build a house (structure) strong enough to stand.

This truth is also found in Matthew 16, where Jesus asks His disciples, "who do you say that I am?" (16:15). Peter gets revelation of Jesus as the Christ. Jesus affirms Peter and says, "Blessed are you, Simon Barjona, because flesh and blood did not reveal this to you, but My Father who is in heaven." (16:17) He's saying, you didn't hear that revelation from anyone else, in the local newspaper, or in a sermon. You heard it straight from heaven. In essence, Simon Peter was being attentive to heaven's voice. He was hearing on a different plain. He was hearing in the spirit. He was picking up what was being announced over Jesus from heaven. It's important to note that Simon's name means "he who hears" while Barjona means "dove." The dove in Scripture signifies Holy Spirit, so his name would translate to "he who hears Holy Spirit." Flesh and blood had nothing to do with this revelation. Peter was hearing in the Spirit.

He then calls him by his other identity and says "you are Peter" (whose name means "rock or stone"). So, when you put this together, we have Jesus rewarding His eager disciple with identity and affirmation. In addition, He's rewarding us (His modern day disciples) with a revelatory message. I can hear the conversation here in Matthew 16 going something like this: "Good job Peter, you've been listening to the voice of my Father. You have a hearing ear. Because you've been hearing in the Spirit, I'm going to raise you up and set your life as an example and a picture of what I will build my church on. I want to build my Kingdom in and through hearers. I want to establish it through those who lean in, listen, and hear the voice of my Father. And through their lives, they will walk in such authority, so much that the very gates of hell won't stand a chance, because they hear a better voice - the voice of my Father." Friends, it's the "Simons" (hearers) through whom He entrusts to establish His Kingdom.

I imagine Peter was stewarding the prayer that Jesus taught them in Matthew 6, when He said "Pray like this, Our Father in heaven…" The Lord's prayer is actually the "ascended prayer," for Jesus was teaching His disciples to pray in the Spirit, from the ascended place of heaven. Even before Jesus teaches them what to pray, He points to whom they're praying. He wanted His people to know that they have a Father in heaven who loves to partner with His children, and it all begins in prayer and by hearing His voice.

So then as we are building, the important question is, "What tools are you using?" It was once said, "as blood is to the body, so communication is to our relationship." The point here is, communication and conversation give life and flow to our relationships. They can't function rightly without it. Therefore, communication is the primary tool in our relationships. This is foundational to understand. Simple yet profound. Obvious yet often overlooked. If we want to build a lasting legacy for the glory of Jesus, we must be hearers - those willing to lean in and commune with the Holy Spirit. We must be willing to stand in the presence of the One, to hear and be quickened by His voice, and just BE. This is the starting point of all "doing." We can't do unless we first be.

> *"Communication is probably the single greatest vehicle of any relationship. Although some people have a problem believing that God wants to talk to everybody, most believers understand that true prayer is not just petitioning Heaven with a list of requests, but is communicating with Him as a true friend."*
>
> – *Basic Training for the Prophetic Ministry* by Kris Vallotton

In light of this, Jesus is inviting us into a life of prayer. To the Master Builder, it's the most basic tool in our journey. It is the basic and fundamental tool for all other tools to function rightly. Our teaching, missions, and evangelism just won't work without it. So again, what tools are you using? Is prayer your primary?

How ironic would it be for a married couple to never communicate? We might have a few problems, you think? It'd be absurd to think that one could just walk down the aisle of that chapel, say a few words, and never enter into intimate fellowship with his or her spouse. Imagine the months of preparation that the bride goes through to make this day so special, only to say a few words, then part her own way. She orders the flowers, designs the cake, buys the dress, lining up everything according to how she desires, and only gets to enjoy the time together at the altar. Can you just imagine the amount of disaster that would lie ahead?

It would be just as absurd to think that we could function and maintain a vibrant relationship with Jesus without the realm of communication, without prayer. Yet some believers do this. They say the salvation prayer yet never plunge into an intimate walk with the Lord. They stay in "servant" mode and never enter into the friend reality that He's called us to.

Friends, in my opinion, this is one of the greatest losses in the Kingdom of God - when a believer remains docked at the bay of shallow relationship, never entering into the seas of deep and unbroken fellowship with Him. There is a vast sea of the knowledge of God awaiting us. I imagine the sea is God, the wind is the Holy Spirit, and the boat is prayer. You were made to sail the seas of encounter and dive deep in the waters of knowing Him. Take the dive and begin to swim in the ocean of the knowledge of God. You won't regret it.

PRAYER, THE THREAD OF SCRIPTURE

The Bible is a book of prayers. It's one of the main threads of Scripture. The dialogue and conversation between God and man is paramount in it's pages. Prayer is not something that the patriarchs "added" to their daily activity. Beloved, it was the very core of their walk. Abraham talked with God about his fathering of the nations. Moses spoke with Him about the establishment of the law. Hosea dialogued with God about the fate of an adulterous nation. Ezekiel

> *The Scriptures are a glimpse into the exchange of heaven and earth.*

inquired with Yahweh about the destiny of the dry bones. John the beloved interacted with Him about His love and beauty. The list goes on and on. The truth is, every (righteous) story in the word of God has at its core, interaction and conversation with God.

In fact, the word of God is given us to fuel a life of prayer. It provides us with paradigms of a rescued and redeemed life, that we may stand and minister to Him. It's a mirror that shows us His image and our identity so that we can pray with holy perspective. For example, the book of Psalms is filled with awe and splendor of God's beauty, that we may encounter and pray from the knowledge of God. The book of Revelation is full of end-time insight and serves as a prayer manual for the end-time church. The book of Ephesians is a book of identity so that we can pray with confidence. The book of Hebrews is focused on the Son's work as our Great High Priest that we may offer up a pleasing sacrifice with our prayers. Many, many prayers are locked up in its pages, and God inspires us to say and pray its promises back to Him. He wants conversation. He is a God whose "word will not return void" (Isaiah 55:11), and that returning is accomplished by the saints echoing back the word that originated from His mouth.

In a sense, the garden of Eden (in Genesis 1) was a prayer room. In fact, the very act of man's creation began through a prayer meeting. God said, "Let US make man in our image." (Genesis 1:27) In essence, God said to God, let us form ones who mirror us. It was the place of ultimate interaction and unbroken fellowship as

God's presence dwelt with man. The Hebrew word for presence is paniym meaning "face." The garden was "face to face" encounter with God. The Hebrew word for Eden means "delight, pleasure" and points to the fact that delight and pleasure were the fruit of the garden. His presence was there in fullness. David said it this way in Psalm 16:11, "in Your presence (face) is fullness of joy… there are pleasures (the characteristics of Eden) forevermore." We experience delight and pleasure when we interact with the One whose face is full of joy.

It's interesting that just before His betrayal to death, Jesus held a prayer meeting with His Father in the garden. He didn't go around making His last minute visits with friends and family, rather He prayed! He knew those last moments on earth were crucial and He chose to spend time before God in prayer. God was talking to God. He entered the garden to encounter, commune, and dialogue with His Father. Prayer preceded the persecution. In this prayer meeting, Jesus was calling us back to our eternal destiny, to the "garden" of our calling. He was restoring us as a people who bore His image and who carried His glory. He says, "I desire that they be with Me where I am that they may behold My glory." (John 17:24) I can imagine Jesus' prayer sounding something like this, "Father, I want to go back to the garden where there is unbroken fellowship with man, where our people see the manifest glory of who We are." Jesus knelt in the garden (of Gethsemane) asking for the Eden reality to be restored. The Son of God was calling us back to our true identity as friends and companions in His Father's house, and He was doing it by prayer.

Introduction

Paul, possibly the most powerful man (other than Jesus) in the New Testament, demonstrated an intense lifestyle of prayer. (Romans 1:9) In every season of life, he remained in a spirit of prayer: "...<u>without ceasing</u> I make mention of you always in <u>my prayers</u>." (Ephesians 1:16) "<u>Cease not</u>... making mention of you in <u>my prayers</u>." (Philippians 1:3, 4) "<u>Always in every prayer</u> of mine for you all making request with joy." (Colossians 1:9) "... since the day we heard it, (I) <u>do not cease to pray</u> for you…" (Philemon 4) "... making mention of you <u>always in my prayers</u>." (2 Timothy 1:3) "...<u>without ceasing</u> I have remembrance of you in <u>my prayers night and day</u>." It's evident that prayer was central to the apostle's life.

The early church of Acts operated out of a lifestyle of prayer. It was at their very core. The powerful community was actually one massive corporate prayer meeting which manifested in signs, wonders, and miracles. As a praying people, they would become a church who turned the world upside down (Acts 17:6)… "And they <u>continued steadfastly... in prayers</u>." (Acts 2:42) "These all <u>continued with one accord in prayer</u> and supplication…" (Acts 1:14) "but we will <u>devote ourselves to prayer</u>, and to the ministry of the word." (Acts 6:4) "...but <u>prayer was made without ceasing</u> of the church unto God for him." (Acts 12:5, 12) "Ye also helping together <u>by prayer for us</u>…" (2 Corinthians 1:11).

Cornelius, one of the vessels to usher the Gentile people into the Kingdom, was a man of prayer. It says that he was "a devout man who… <u>prayed to God continually</u>." (Acts 10:2) He prayed to God continually! Just like Paul, he remained in a spirit of prayer, meaning everything he did came out of the place of prayer. This tells us something. God didn't just put the Gentile race into the

> I would rather be more powerful before God in the place of prayer, than before men in ministry.

hands of any individual. He entrusted their destiny to a praying man! Perhaps God knew that He needed to birth this (desire for the Gentiles) into the heart of a man who would continually take them up (in prayer) for the rest of his days. He wanted to birth and sustain this people in prayer.

> *"Rejoice always, pray continually, give thanks in all circumstances; for this is God's will for you in Christ Jesus."*
>
> *– 1 Thessalonians 5:16-18 (NASB)*

WHEN YOU PRAY

In Matthew 6, Jesus gives us the sermon on the Mount. He teaches what many scholars call the "constitution of the Kingdom" and provides ways to walk out the principles found in it. I call them the "when-yous" of the Kingdom, and in these "when-yous," Jesus gives the essentials of walking with Him. He said "when you pray… when you fast… when you give." As gateways to enter into Kingdom lifestyle, the Son of Man presents dynamics that can't just be considered, but ones that must be embraced and lived out. To Jesus, they aren't recommendations, but rather mandatory dynamics that must be adopted. It's prayer, giving, and fasting. (Matthew 6:2-8, 16-18) He didn't say, "Try this and hopefully it works. If it doesn't, you can go back to business as usual." No… He said "when you." He expected His church to pursue nothing more and nothing less than a vibrant life of interaction with the Father. He demonstrated a life of prayer and expected His disciples to do the same.

When the disciples wanted to grow in the things of God, they didn't ask Him how to preach, sing, nor how to administrate, not even how to be a more effective minister. They asked Jesus how to pray. (Luke 11:1) The disciples connected the power of Jesus with the prayer life of Jesus. They experienced Him raising the dead, opening the blind eyes, and preaching the Kingdom with signs and wonders. They had seen Him lay hands on the sick and have them quickly recover. As they beheld this Man from Nazareth demonstrating such power, they quickly connected the works to His prayer life.

CHANGING US AND CHANGING THINGS

It's amazing that prayer can both change things as it can also change us to change things. They are both equally true. I have seen both dynamics come alive many times. Interestingly, I've even heard saints argue the effects of prayer, where one camp leans toward sitting before the Lord and praying for many hours in a specific location. This camp believes that the longer you sit before the Lord in prayer, the greater breakthrough one will experience. I've also seen the camps where they spend little time in corporate prayer but much time doing evangelism (foot work). This camp believes that prayer must have "ready feet". One says, "You must spend many hours in intercession, laboring continuously for the souls of men," while the other says, "Yeah, but I don't have to spend hours doing so, there's work to be done!". (Both camps are sincere and have a heart to see Jesus glorified). You're probably laughing right now, as you see yourself in one of the two.

My opinion is, we shouldn't argue about it. They are both equally true. I don't think we have to pick. Prayer changes things as it also changes us to change things. There is however, a divine order that God has given for us to follow. It's a proven design that He's set up. We see it in the story of Jehoshaphat. This particular account would set a precedent for the people of God throughout history. 2 Chronicles 20 tells us that the armies of Israel were pressing in on every side and they needed breakthrough. The king was afraid but God wasn't, for He had a solution. To summarize the story, Jehoshaphat first sought the Lord, by establishing prayer and praise on the frontline. Very unconventional to the human mind, it was his first move. The writer tells us that the enemy soon turned on themselves.

> *"As they began to sing and praise, the Lord set ambushes against the men… and they were defeated."*
>
> — 2 Chronicles 20:22 (NASB)

Yes, they defeated themselves. What a strategy! Although there are many hidden truths here, the obvious is this - God is enthroned on the praises (melodic prayers) of His people. When we establish an altar of praise and prayer, He establishes His strength in our midst. Most kings would have gone straight to the generals and rallied the troops. But here we have the wisest move. Establish the intercession with worshippers up front and God will fight! If we're going to launch weaponry, let's (first) do it with that of praise and prayer!

> *"Evangelism without intercession is like an explosive without a detonator."*
>
> — *First of All… Intercession* by Reinhard Bonnke

Introduction

It was at a worship service that Jesus commanded us to "go into all the world" (Matthew 28:17). Out of encounter with the glory of the Lord, Isaiah said, "Here am I, send me." (Isaiah 6:8) The Great Commission (to go into all the world) should always be received and established in the place of prayer.

One of the most obvious of these two dynamics coming together is the bringing in of revival. Some camps will say, "We need to pray more and harder for revival," while the other camps will say, " We need to demonstrate revival and go into the world, preaching the gospel." Both camps think that they are right. They will both declare it until they're blue in the face. Well, I have good news. Both are true and right. Nevertheless, the application of prayer (intercession) and evangelism isn't about separation, but about sequence. Remember, Holy Spirit gave the apostles tongues of fire. From the place of upper room waiting, He released blazing prayer and fiery intercession. From the platform of fiery prayer, He would send them preaching and proclaiming the gospel. The sequence was pray then preach, pray some more, then preach some more. The two were to go together.

> *The application of prayer (intercession) and evangelism isn't about separation, but about sequence.*

THERE'S PROOF

One of the clearest examples of intercession and evangelism working together is in Reinhard Bonnke's ministry. As you may know, Bonkke conducts large crusades in much of Africa and has seen multitudes of salvations, healing, signs and wonders since the 60's. Records (by decision cards) indicate that his ministry has seen salvations in the 73 million range (from CfaN website October 2015). Yes, I said 73 million! Now that's some effective ministry!

Reinhard studied at The Bible College of Wales, where he was deeply impacted by its director and founder Samuel Rees Howell, who received a strong legacy of intercession from his father Rees Howell (1879-1950). He was known as an avid preacher and intercessor. Intercession was his defining message. One of Rees' books "A Life of Intercession" has become a timeless classic on the subject. The legacy of prayer and intercession on this man's life is so powerful, that there have been four prominent biographies written on it (Rees Howell Intercessor; The Intercession of Rees Howell; Samuel Rees Howell: A Life of Intercession; Samuel, Son, and Successor of Rees Howell).

Bonnke says this about his crusades, "All our campaigns are conducted under a great canopy consisting of weeks of prayer. Prayer builds a roof over us that shuts out any devil." Not a few hours or even a few days of prayer, but "weeks of prayer." An article from his ministry (CfaN) website boasts the proof of prayer in every evangelistic campaign.

> "Every evangelistic campaign begins with intensive prayer. Before the location of the next major gospel outreach is selected, Reinhard Bonnke, the CfaN management and the campaign organizers together seek the Lord and allow him to give them directions. When a particular location has been determined, the preparation team travels there. A committee of local pastors and leaders wishing to

involve their church fellowships in the campaign is set up. A few weeks before the start of the meetings other CfaN Team members visit the churches to instruct them in intercession and to create a prayer base in advance of the gospel campaign. However, during the services intensive prayer is also made for a victorious breakthrough of the gospel. Reinhard Bonnke is convinced that an evangelistic campaign without permanent accompanying prayer is like a bomb without a detonator."

We see that the art of intercession has had a profound impact on the life and ministry of this great evangelist. It shows us the key is to create a prayer base in advance of the gospel. Both intercession and evangelism are to work together. They go hand in hand. Like "73 million salvations" type of working together. You can't argue with this type of lasting and fruitful impact. Bonkke continues to say that he sees Africa being washed in the blood of the Lamb, referring to a vision given to him in his early years - a "blood-washed" Africa. I've even heard Bonkke talk about his team of intercessors praying in the Spirit (together in a concentrated place) while he preaches. At one time, they were stationed underneath the elevated stage. He understood that his preaching must go forth in clear air if it were to be effective, and the only way was through the air assault of intercession.

> *"It's pray and go, pray and go, pray and go, and pray and preach."*
>
> – Reinhard Bonkke (from IHOP-KC article)

Just imagine, a few weeks of laboring in intercession results in whole villages coming to Jesus. One four-day crusade in Zumbia reported a total of 384,110 registered decision cards. That's an average of 96,000 decisions a day. What a return! This is the power of intercession and evangelism working together for the greater cause of Jesus receiving the rewards of His suffering.

Now, while I use large numbers to prove a point here, I don't want you to solely focus on that. Many of us may never be able to preach to large crowds like this, and that's fine. The main point here is, when intercession and evangelism come together (either in your own personal life or in a massive crusade), we have fruitful and lasting impact. The two never war against each other, and should always be coupled to bring the greater cause of glorifying Jesus. Reinhard says, "Evangelism without prayer is like an explosive without a detonator, and prayer without evangelism is like a detonator without an explosive. We need both." Thinking they are separable is like saying that the engine of a car is more valuable than the transmission, or vice versa. Both are valuable for getting the job done. The engine creates the fire and spark, while the transmission signifies the moving forward. If you don't have the two working together, you won't get very far!

Another example is in the ministry and life of Charles Finney, a fiery evangelist from Connecticut. Giving up legal practice as an attorney to preach the gospel, Finney was well known for his fervent pursuit of God. Following a life-changing encounter with God, Finney returned to his law office to meet with a client whose case he was about to argue. "I have a retainer from the Lord Jesus Christ to plead His cause," he told the man, "and cannot plead yours." From that point, he stepped into being a revivalist of his day. Many historians call him the "father of modern revivalism," noting that he paved the way for subsequent renowned evangelists like Billy Sunday, D.L. Moody, and Billy Graham. One article tells of his revival spirit:

> *"Finney seemed so anointed with the Holy Spirit that people were often brought under conviction of sin just by looking at him. When holding meetings at Utica, New York, he visited a large factory. At the sight of him one of the workers, and then another, and then another broke down and wept under a sense of their sins, and finally so many were sobbing and weeping that the machinery had to be stopped while Finney pointed them to Christ."*
>
> *— Charles G. Finney* by David Smithers

When one looks into Finney's life, you will find a deep commitment to prayer and intercession. Much like Reinhard, he wouldn't even preach until he felt that the strongholds of that area were diminished. He knew that if his preaching was to go forth with power, he had to have open air, prepared by the ministry of intercession. Later in his ministry, Finney employed two men to help carry the torch of intercession. Their names were Father Nash and Abel Clary. These men would partner and labor in prayer for Finney's meetings and goings, until they felt that breakthrough occurred. They laid the foundation in much of the revivals that we read about. These weren't men who had a timid prayer life, but were ones given wholly to the place of prayer and intercession. It was their occupation. With a spirit of prayer, both men would keep a prayer list and journal to log Finney's ministry, as they continually covered him in prayer.

Many have called Father Nash the secret of Finney's ministry. I guess you could say, behind the revivals and the multitudes coming to Jesus under this ministry, was a man tucked away in his room (or the woods), clearing the air for the gospel message to go forth. One report said that often before daybreak, you could hear Father Nash for nearly half a mile away crying out in deep prayer. The sense of God's presence was overwhelming around this man. Finney himself wrote of Clary saying, "Mr. Clary continued as long as I did, and he did not leave until after I had left. He never appeared in public, but he gave himself wholly to prayer. Clary had been licensed to preach; but his spirit of prayer was such, he was so burdened with the souls of men, that he was not able to preach much, his whole time and strength being given to prayer." From New York City revivals to Ohio outbreaks, prayer is found threading throughout it all.

> "The zenith of Finney's evangelistic career was reached at Rochester, New York, where he preached 98 sermons between September 10, 1830, and March 6, 1831. Shopkeepers closed their businesses, posting notices urging people to attend Finney's meetings. Reportedly, the population of the town increased by two-thirds during the revival, but crime dropped by two-thirds over the same period."
>
> – *Christianty Today* article on Charles Finney

Every authentic revival has always had at its core, a praying people. On the other hand, every revival has also had at the heart, a yielded vessel(s). In fact, when these two dynamics come together, you have an explosion. When you can get a people praying who are also postured to move and obey, it's bad news for the kingdom of darkness. So, I say let's do both. Let's do Joel 2 (by waiting on the Lord in the place of prayer), then be willing to obey quickly at the sound of His voice. Let's cry out for the fire and stand willing to be the sacrifice. Remember, it was Isaiah who (out of the place of encounter and fellowship with the Lord) said "here am I, send me." (Isaiah 6:8) You can't encounter the Lord and not develop a burning and compassionate heart for the gospel. It's just not possible.

> *Behind the visible outpourings of revival, one can hear the rumblings of prayer and intercession. The platform of power is built by a praying people.*

> *"Prayer is never an acceptable substitute for obedience. The sovereign Lord accepts no offering from His creatures that is not accompanied by obedience. To pray for revival while ignoring or actually flouting the plain precept laid down in the Scriptures is to waste a lot of words and get nothing for our trouble."*
>
> – A.W. Tozer

BE READY AT ALL TIMES

For me, I don't like to minister unless I've first spent some valuable time in prayer. Whether I'm leading worship or teaching, I like to take at least 20-30 minutes to slow down and engage my mind with the Lord in personal worship and prayer. Most of the time I pray in the Spirit and connect my heart to who He is, mediating on His goodness and reminding myself of His nature. It's nothing "epic" or groundbreaking when I do it, but it's subtle little reminders to my heart that He is good. When I teach Sundays, I have the luxury of being covered in prayer by my team of intercessors.

However, there are other times where a situation arises that we don't have time to get away and quiet our mind. I call them "Holy Spirit moments." There are those times when at Wal-Mart, the Holy Spirit prompts you to pray for the lady in the entryway. It's when you're in the grocery aisle and He puts that sick person in your path to lay hands on for healing. It's those moments. They're all around us. You see, I believe that every Christian is a minister in some form or fashion, in whatever sphere He has you in. You don't need a pulpit or a pew, nor does it require a worship band or a congregation. All you need is Holy Spirit and a willing heart. He just seems to view every venue as a place for potential ministry. With that said, I strongly believe every believer should be living out the gospel in everyday life. It may be at the workplace, in the grocery store, at school, the doctor's office, at church, or at home. Whatever it looks like, the Holy Spirit wants us to be ready at all times. He wants us on guard and armed with the love of God in every situation. Paul told Timothy, "preach the word; be ready in season and out of season…" (2 Timothy 4:2)

As I said earlier, there are times when the Holy Spirit calls on us to minister on the spot to someone and we just don't have the time to get away and quiet our mind. These opportunities call for immediate action. So, I believe it's crucial that the church operate in a spirit of prayer - the kind of prayer lifestyle that Paul urged us in when he said to "pray without ceasing." (1 Thessalonians 5:17) You see, he wasn't saying that our lips had to be moving all day, rather he was urging the believers to keep their minds and hearts engaged with God - to remain in a mode of fellowship with God. This means that we continually meditate on His nature and what He's saying. It's ongoing communion and conversation from a quiet heart. In any case, the Holy Spirit wants us to have our antennas up! Remaining in a spirit of prayer can be applied by praying under your breath as you work, meditating on the Word, or thinking on a certain attribute of God. Or if you work a job where you're constantly having to interact with people, it's about keeping your heart in tune with what the Lord is saying to those around you. Having a spirit of prayer is about being God-conscious at all times and responding with a ready heart. In fact, having this mindset and heart attitude will result in increased prayer and conversation with God. The one complements the other.

THE HIGH CALLING OF PRAYER

I often refer to prayer as our high calling. It is the very means by which we interact with Him and release His resources into the earth. Our high calling isn't about having the biggest church or the most influential ministry. Many seek these things, but I've learned that this is not true success, nor is it the way to lasting joy. Friends, there is no shortcut to enjoying fellowship with God. Fellowship is centered around the idea of actually spending time with Him and talking to Him.

> *"Being with Him is just the most sure way to recognize His voice."*
>
> — Rick Joyner

One of the primary reasons for Jesus' descending to planet earth was to make His home inside of us. He wanted His Spirit to dwell in the frame of those who call on Him. It was about being able to abide in a people. He wanted unbroken fellowship. We see this in the prayer that Jesus prayed before being led to the cross…

> *"Father, I desire that they also, whom You have given Me, be with Me where I am, so that they may see My glory which You have given Me…"*
>
> – John 17:24

The Godhead wasn't content with merely living "upon" a people, He wanted to dwell in the inward parts of them. He desired closeness and as Jonathan David Helser writes, "He's closer than the skin on our bones… closer than the wind in our lungs." Jesus made a way that He may speak directly to our soul and that we may experience Him at any time. He dwells in His people and His people dwell in Him. It's Christ in us the hope of glory (Colossians 1:27), and us in Him, the only hope for justification and redemption. (2 Corinthians 5:17) At this point, we become one. This my friends, is a paramount desire of God.

two

My Own Story

Growing up in church and tent meetings, I was familiar with the activity of prayer. As the child of a devout man of God and the grandson of a fiery Southern Baptist preacher, the idea of having a prayer life was nothing new. I practically grew up beneath a church pew, so in my head I knew one must pray. In my heart, my actions spoke otherwise. Although I knew that prayer was important and was a value of the Christian life, I never realized the absolute necessity of prayer. Until later in life, I only saw it as a supplement to our walk with the Lord, failing to realize that it was the very fabric in our journey with God.

However, God in His great leadership and mercy, has been so faithful in my journey. He has been so patient to wait in my presence, hearing me pray for things I already have, beg for things I didn't, lead misguided prayer meetings, pray misquoted Scripture, and even doze off at times. I've definitely experienced many things in prayer that one should not do. I know you're probably laughing right now, but it's the truth. My journey of prayer has not been an easy one. It has been nothing but weak and frail at times. However, I'm so glad that I stuck with it. The many hours of "sweating it out" pales in comparison to the many encounters I've experienced during these times. Some of the encounters were more subtle while some were more dramatic, yet they've brought me to the place I am today. So, what you're reading is an account of my journey in prayer. This is my story…

HEARING THOSE PRAYERS

At a young age, I remember being told that prayer was the key to all success and breakthrough. And growing up in a godly home, I not only heard it, but I experienced it firsthand. I can almost recite the prayers that my little ears heard, especially the prayers of my mom and grandma. They both were and still are praying women. It was in that little house in Eubank, Kentucky, on those early mornings, that I remember my mother faithfully praying the word over my brother and me as we got ready for school, and it wasn't just before school, it was on the way to our basketball games, just before those grueling exams, in route to the high school golf matches in the family vehicle, etc. In essence, I grew up in a prayer-saturated home. If anyone was ever sick or stressed, you were going to hear mom or dad declaring the word over you. I remember prayers like "I thank You Lord that my children are blessed coming in and going out. I thank You that my children are the head and not the tail, above and not beneath.

Cultivate prayer, for the next generation is listening… Soon, those prayers will become batons in their hands.

Lord, You have anointed them to walk in divine wisdom." I could go on and on with the prayers that I heard and how they still to this day, continue to stand for our family. In fact, many of the prayers that were spoken over me have become bombs of blessing that I now release over my own children.

EYEWITNESS OF BREAKTHROUGH IN PRAYER

One of the breakthroughs of prayer that I clearly remember was when my grandpa was diagnosed with an aneurism. It was 1989 and I was only 8 years old at the time. However, I'll never forget this amazing account of God's faithfulness. The report of the doctor was that he had only months to live. The artery had expanded to such a size, they didn't know what to do, so they sent him home with a hopeless report. Things seemed to look pretty grim as he realized he only had a few months to enjoy his family and friends. However, what some of us failed to realize, was there was a woman on the other end who heard a different report. She had a revelation of the Lord's will over my grandfather's life and knew that he wasn't finished fulfilling his mandate in this life. She heard a different report, but it wasn't the report of the earthly doctor. Friends, it was the report of the Lord. This lady was my grandmother, Joyce Atwood.

So from the day they received the report, she determined to bombard heaven with the report of the Lord. It happened to be an ancient report called "Psalm 91." This Psalm is packed with declarations of the Lord's provision and protection over His children. It's a promise of divine covering to those who abide in the "shadow of the Almighty." So, every morning and many times throughout the day, she would call upon heaven for the healing and preservation of Adlai Atwood. To this day, I remember hearing her quote that 16 verse Psalm like it was her own. To my grandma, it was Adlai's prescription. She didn't back up nor did she give in, but with the persistence of Hannah (who birthed Samuel), she pressed into this ancient promise: "This I declare about the Lord: He alone is my refuge, my place of safety; He is my God, and I trust Him. For He will rescue you from every trap and protect you from deadly disease. He will cover you with his feathers. He will shelter you with his wings. His faithful promises are your armor and protection." (Psalm 91:3, 4)

After faithfully praying this verse every morning, my grandpa Adlai Atwood, lived for another 12 years. Yes, another 12 years! Not another year or even 6 years, 12 years! What seemed to be a 6 month hopeless report, turned into another decade of experiencing the faithfulness of God. My grandpa went on to preach many more revivals and meetings, running hard after the Lord. We became eyewitnesses to the power of His word through prayer. This testimony is forever burned into the hearts of our family and friends who were eyewitnesses of this miracle.

I also specifically remember some of my papaws (Adlai Atwood) tent meetings, where in one particular meeting in Stanford KY, a man who had been partially blind for most of his life came forward for prayer. Sitting on the ground on that warm summer night, I remember looking up to see my grandpa remove the mans glasses and then pray for him. Although I couldn't make out the words, I understood that papaw was praying for healing. This was common for my papaw, so I didn't think much about it. However, what happened next was enough to make a person run the aisles (yeah, I grew up Pentecostal). Removing his hands from the man's eyes, my papaw then asked the man to walk to the opposite end of the tent, which was probably 50 feet away. When the man made it to the end, Adlai instructed the man to call back the number of fingers that he was holding up. This was asking the impossible, since the man was now without glasses and could barely see his own hand in front of him. Amazingly, the man begins to call out one by one, the numbers on my papaw's hand. As he called out the numbers with such gladness, it was evident that this man was fully healed, and the crowd soon erupted with celebration of the man who had just received his sight. This is one of those Holy Spirit moments where I was marked by the power of prayer, specifically the prayer of faith and healing.

Oh the effects of hearing these prayers at such a young age. The seeds that they planted will be forever remembered in my heart. Although I witnessed many breakthroughs of prayer, the Lord would soon make prayer a personal expression. I would begin to experience the breakthroughs on my own. I'll share those later on in this chapter.

A SHIFT IN MY LIFE

It was February 2006 when things began to drastically change for me. From this day forward, my life would never be the same, especially related to prayer. It was Valentine's Day and I was driving to Cincinnati for work, listening to a teaching by Lou Engle on "governmental prayer." In declaring that the Lord was raising up the praying church, Lou uses this term "house of prayer." For those of you who know of Lou Engle, you'll know what I mean when I say that what he said was with force and authority. Upon saying the phrase "house of prayer," my heart came alive. I had heard this phrase preached by many a preacher, but this time something was different. Something had finally connected. It's like when he said the phrase, my heart came alive in a way I had never experienced before. You see, some months before this (in the fall of 2005), the Lord had been dealing with me about a passage in Psalm 127 - "Unless the Lord builds the house." For several months, the verse had been consuming me. I would read it several times a day, pray into it, meditate on it, and even study it. I'd wake up and go to bed thinking about it, and knew that the Lord was saying something in it, just not exactly sure what. It wasn't long before I wrote a song called "God's Building a House," declaring the truth of it. I knew there was a house He was building and He was going to do it.

Wrestling with the meaning of this verse months leading up to this day, it all finally began to make sense. On this day in February, I began to understand that the "house" which he had been speaking to me about was the house of prayer. He was raising up the house of prayer and I was going to partner with Him somehow and some way to build it. To make a long story short, on that February morning, I said yes to this calling to raise up the house of prayer.

To be quite honest, when I heard this call to build the house of prayer, I didn't understand fully what the Lord was saying. I was "smart enough" to understand that it was a place of prayer (hence the name), but that was about the extent of it. At this moment, I was very limited in my view of prayer, much less the establishing of a ministry founded upon it. To say the least, I had a long way to go.

THE JOURNEY BEGINS

After hearing the Lord call me to this "house of prayer," I felt it was necessary to submit it to a few of my spiritual fathers, one being my pastor at that time. I shared the brief overview of what the Lord had revealed and wanted to get his covering in prayer and encouragement. To my surprise, I walked out of his office in charge of the prayer ministry, not because I wanted to take over the prayer ministry, but because the Lord knew that He had to throw me into it. He knew I had just enough zeal to say yes, but not enough wisdom to launch it. The Lord used him to throw me into the water that day, and it was either sink or swim. I left the pastor's office thinking, "What just happened?" I simply wanted to get some wisdom and instruction of how to handle this word, yet I left in charge of a prayer ministry. This is not what I envisioned up front. Oh, the Lord in His wisdom and humor! To say the least, this would be the beginning of a great journey of leaning on Him and learning how to pray.

I figured if I was going to lead a prayer ministry, it would be a good idea that I learn how to pray myself, especially that I would enjoy it. You see, when I heard the Lord call me to build a house of prayer on that February morning, I really didn't enjoy prayer very much. I definitely knew one must pray and did so myself, but at the time I had little burning passion for it. In my eyes, I wasn't the "prime candidate" to lead a prayer ministry. Oh, but the Lord in His wisdom and humor! He does things like this to prove His goodness, and my life stands as a testimony of how the Lord, in His patience, can use weak and frail people.

LEARNING TO PRAY

In my eagerness to begin this journey of learning to pray, I decided to sit under a few people who actually knew how to pray. I figured this was the best way to get trained. For weeks, I would walk into our church's prayer room with a couple of the praying men from the church. Among these men was my dad Carson Atwood and a good friend, Dennis Nartker. I would listen to these men of God pray, take notes, and then add to what I was hearing. I figured if I could just repeat some of the same things I was hearing, it would be okay. I would think, "That sounds good," so I would inject my own passion for the Lord with the phrases, and it actually started working. These men are men of the Word, so anything they were declaring was usually right on. Several weeks went by and before I knew it, I was enjoying prayer. It wasn't long that I would even get excited before each prayer meeting. Many times, I remember actually looking forward to the prayer meetings. This thing was starting to form into more than just a discipline, Prayer was becoming a delight. I was thinking, "Wow, prayer is actually enjoyable!" During this time, prayer was becoming more about encountering a Person than it was about sustaining a habit. I realized I was actually talking to a real Person on a real throne who loved me, who delighted in me, and actually longed to answer me (more than I longed to be heard). Beloved, this truth and revelation began to change everything. It was touching every part of my life. It was evident that the Lord was up to something in this season. Looking back, I was becoming a house of prayer.

During this time, I launched One27 House of Prayer there in the local church, as it ran alongside and served the vision of the house. In a period of 3 1/2 years, we raised up several weekly on-campus

> *When you begin to understand that you're dialoguing with the King of the earth, it changes everything. When you see that He desires your partnership in the place of prayer, you talk about experiencing a new realm of prayer.*

prayer meetings, many prayer walks, hosted two regional conferences, and raised up many corporate worship and prayer gatherings. I had many good laborers in prayer, as they helped build a culture of worship and prayer. In 2011, I stepped out and launched One27 as a house of prayer that functioned in its own location. We first launched One27 in London, KY, where we went strong for 2 years, as I served alongside some amazing people to host many worship and prayer meetings with teaching. After serving in London for those 2 years, we felt the Lord calling us to put down our stakes in Somerset, KY, in January of 2013.

I now lead a thriving house of prayer in Southeast Kentucky, where we have several hours of worship and prayer going on throughout the week. I serve as lead director of One27 and I love my job. We are building a culture of worship and prayer by regular prayer meetings, while enjoying the benefits of it with thriving community and effective outreach. I've seen firsthand how He's taken fragmented pieces of my journey and formed a tapestry of love and delight of prayer. Even though there are still many challenges to building a prayer culture, I'm having a blast. In terms of ministry, it's my primary passion in life. Whether I'm encountering Jesus on those early mornings in my office or leading prayer meetings at One27, I stand as a testimony of His goodness in the place of prayer.

I've definitely learned some valuable lessons. I've learned what worked and what didn't, and will continue to learn these things. I've personally come into contact with the delight as well as the drudgery of prayer, experiencing firsthand the joys as well as the disasters of leading prayer meetings. There have been several prayer meetings where we left full of excitement about what the Lord was doing and there were others where we wondered if He was even in the same neighborhood. I remember one prayer meeting in particular where a lady began to prophesy and pray some of the goofiest things you can possibly imagine, on the mic. Then there was that prayer meeting where the open mic prayer time turned into a "preachathon." For some reason, there are those who think open prayer is their "time to shine." (That kind of meeting actually happened several times).

As you can probably see, my journey hasn't been the smoothest or the most enjoyable, but boy has it been worth it. There have been times where I left prayer meetings discouraged and thinking "Why have you called me to this type of ministry Lord?" There were other moments when it would've been easier just to give up and hand it over to someone else. But it was in those difficult times that I decided to stick it out. Looking back, the Lord was so faithful to lead me in my journey. It's almost like He wouldn't let me give up. By His goodness, I just continued to show up and say yes. It may have been a weak "yes" that I was giving Him, but it was a yes. In those times, it wasn't long before the Lord led me into a fresh encounter. For example, He has used a prophetic number (127) over the last decade. It has appeared hundreds of times, to remind my heart that He's in this. He is more involved in the details than I even realize. He was enjoying the journey the whole time and wanted me to. He wasn't giving up and was urging me to do the same. Working behind the scenes in the places I didn't immediately recognize, I now see all of these hurdles as a form of His grace. He's "Jehovah-sneaky!"

With all these various dynamics and emotions, I'm glad I decided to stick it out. I now stand as a witness to the faithfulness of God in the place of prayer. In my decade of leaning and leading in prayer, He continues to spur me on to remain faithful and constant. No matter what season we're in or what ministry we're involved with, faithfulness is one of the universal encouragements of the Holy Spirit. It's an attribute that pays great dividends, as I have seen firsthand in engaging in a life of prayer. Here are a few testimonies in my journey.

PERSONAL BREAKTHROUGHS OF PRAYER

One of the personal breakthroughs I experienced was in 2008 with the birth of our little girl Olivia. As we load up the bags and get ready to head home from the hospital room, the nurse in charge of accounts walks in and asks how we are going to pay for the delivery and our stay at the hospital. Thinking we have maternity coverage, I reply that we have insurance and will pay the deductible, to which she replies that we have no maternity coverage. You can just imagine the amount of shock, especially when she told us the amount. It had several zeros. No coverage… somehow when filling out our insurance form, we had not checked the little box for that specific coverage. Oops! So, here we are holding a sizable bill, and I mean sizable, like upwards of $11,000! After I work out of the anxiety and stress of it all some days later, I begin to ask the Lord for favor and just plain help. In the natural, I know it could take us a long time to knock this bill out, possibly years. So, I begin to ask for supernatural favor. I even call on some of my closest friends who know the situation and ask that they agree with me for breakthrough. To make a long story short, after some prayer and communication with the hospital, I march down to the account office to try and settle this account. They had asked that I come in so we could discuss their payment plans. I was a bit nervous, yet also a bit expectant, since this situation had been covered in much prayer. To say the least, it was a day of great breakthrough. As the supervisor asked a few questions, she looked at me and said, "we never do this type of discount, but Mr. Atwood, we're going to cut this bill down 80 percent." She and I both were taken aback. In fact, she even pulled the note with the amount written on it and checked the numbers again. It's almost like she was stunned at her own action to cut the bill nearly $9,000. The other part of this is, I had just enough (from our tax return) to pay the bill in full that day. What started out as a financial disaster soon turned into an amazing breakthrough.

Soon after this, my wife and I went through some tough financial struggles. We had just bought a new house and settled in, when all of a sudden I lost my job. We'd adjusted our lifestyle around this job and all of this was amidst our newborn baby girl Olivia. Trying to get back to work, I approached several employers but the doors kept getting closed. For weeks, I was under some immense pressure! There was one client that I pursued heavily, but I just couldn't get him to accept my offer - it was his way or no way and at the time, I wasn't able to comply to his expectations. However, just coming out of the "hospital bill breakthrough," I decided to go on a 21-day Daniel fast with focused prayer. Day 1 of the fast, I remember sitting at my desk in sheer desperation and with tears in my eyes, I poured out my heart before the Lord, asking for financial breakthrough. I was staking my claim that day as I journaled my desperate request to the Lord. I was looking to Him for provision. I wasn't for sure how He was going to do it, but I knew He'd been faithful up to this point, so I just leaned in. It was a weak lean, but at least it was one in the right direction. To make a longer story short, on day 3 He answered with clear breakthrough. That day the owner of the business I had been trying to hire as a client approached me out of the blue and agreed to hire me as a buyer for his company. This was huge! Keep in mind, he boldly denied me weeks leading up to this. He was a stern man and was known for making clear cut choices and not turning back. Yet, he approached me and agreed to work together. Talk about major breakthrough.

Once at the end of a revival service, I began to feel a real burden for a lady in the third row. Not knowing her, all I could hear was "her mother is going to be okay." Little did I know that she had been struggling with crippling fear that her mother was going to die. She had been hospitalized under some serious conditions and it looked dim for the family. I called her up front and spoke a short, simple prayer of peace over her and at that moment, every weight of oppression and fear broke. I backed it up with the word that the Lord had given me earlier. Soon, peace filled that room and what she had been carrying for weeks, was now handed over to the Lord. The Holy Spirit will often well up in us a word that He wants released in prayer.

Just recently we were in a corporate worship and prayer service, where we prayed for eyes and ears to be opened to the knowledge of God. It was a powerful time in the Lord! Shortly after the set, a young girl came up to me for prayer. She expressed her desire to see the Lord break in with answers to some of her questions. She had reached a point of testing in her faith and was asking for breakthrough in her "knower." I asked her if there was anything else she was desiring to see the Lord do in her life, upon which she replied "Yes, I need healing in my left ear." She told me of how she had lost hearing in most of her left ear and was at the point of surgery or having a hearing aid installed. I felt like the Lord wanted to answer her doubt and current season of shaking with gospel power and the demonstration of His love for her. As I laid my hand on her left ear, I sensed this phrase, "From debating to demonstration." In that moment, I knew that the Lord wanted to demonstrate His love for this young 12 year old daughter of God, by releasing healing to her. As soon as I finished praying, I snapped my fingers in her left ear and asked her if she could hear. She nodded yes and I asked her again in a more serious manner. At that moment, her eyes filled with tears as she realized she was hearing sounds in that ear she had not heard in months. Friends, this young girl experienced the breaking in of God's Kingdom. The next day, her mother rushed her to the doctor and confirmed that she had indeed regained 100% hearing in her left ear. Come on Jesus!

What started out as a prayer meeting for the church to regain sight and hearing in the knowledge of God, soon turned into a demonstration of the Lord restoring physical hearing to a near-deaf ear. What a joy it is to partner with Jesus in prayer, and to make the wrong things right. He wants to demonstrate His love in such powerful ways, and He is looking for a people who will but open their mouth and release it wherever they go.

three
Praying from Identity

I love the confidence that Jesus walked in when He was on the earth. He spoke with so much authority that "the crowds were amazed at his teaching, because He taught as one who had authority, and not as their teachers of the law." (Matthew 7:28-29) When He walked onto the scene, demons ran from Him while the hungry clung to Him. He says that He did nothing but what He saw the Father doing. (John 5:19) Jesus was a walking image of God the Father. This tells me that all of Jesus' doing was from the place of seeing the Father's goodness over mankind. God dwelt in pure light and Jesus brought that light to the earth. Having the confidence that He was God's favorite, He lived from the eternal resources of heaven as a Son - One completely loved and accepted by His Father. His identity was Sonship and He lived from that place. He didn't spend 3 decades on the earth trying to figure out who He was. Jesus knew who He was and whose He was. It was His identity. All of His doing came from His being. This is how the Father wants us to live.

The enemy wants to keep us from living a life of prayer, and will go to great lengths to keep us arm's length from the promises of God and our identity in Him. He'll get us busy and bored, disengaged and dead, all to keep us from our purpose of fellowship with God. He knows if he can keep us from having ongoing conversation with our Father, he can keep us from understanding our identity and ultimately our destiny. Revelation 12:10 says that satan accuses us day and night, working overtime to distort our view of God and destroy our destiny. He knows once we get a revelation of Christ and His beauty, it will usher us into a revelation of who we are in Him, and that's where identity comes alive. Once we see Him, we begin to see ourselves more clearly.

As we understand our place in Him, we can begin to pray from our identity in Christ - not merely for it. It's crucial to understand that we are seated, clothed, and given His resources to release over whatever we are praying for. He has blessed us with every spiritual blessing in Christ. (Ephesians 1:3) We can release joy into a barren place because we have joy living in us; we can break the power of darkness because the light dwells inside of us; we can bring calm to the storm around because peace resides in our spirit. The president of the Unites States can sit in his oval office and summon thousands of troops to battle because he is the Commander in Chief. It came with the position. He doesn't have to wonder if he has the power to call on his army, he knows that the job came with the inherit power to drive back the enemies with one important call. The same goes with the believer. We have been given the authority to dispatch angels upon one important call.

Remember in Matthew 16, when Jesus asked the question, "who do you say that I am?" The Creator of the universe wasn't looking for someone to affirm His identity, rather, He was searching and doing inventory of the

The law says you must act a certain way to obtain something. Grace says you have already obtained it, now start praying like it.

disciples' knowledge of God. He wanted to see what their view of Him was. So Peter in his eagerness to speak out, says "You are the Christ, the Son of the Living God." (Matthew 16:16) The young disciple got it right! He picked up on heaven's answer. "Jesus said to him, "Blessed are you, Simon Barjona, because flesh and blood did not reveal this to you, but My Father who is in heaven."

It goes on to tell us that Jesus unloads the young disciple's destiny right there. With an eagerness greater than Simon Peter's, Jesus replies "I also say to you that you are Peter, and upon this rock I will build My church; and the gates of Hades will not overpower it. I will give you the keys of the kingdom of heaven; and whatever you bind on earth shall have been bound in heaven, and whatever you loose on earth shall have been loosed in heaven." (Matthew 16:18, 19) I'm sure Peter and the disciples are thinking, "What just happened?" Peter just happened to answer the question and Jesus reveals his eternal destiny. Friends, this is what happens when we tap into the knowledge of who Jesus is. When we begin to discern and discover the knowledge of God, He answers us with our own identity. As we gaze on Him in prayer, He gives us a glimpse of who we are in Him, and over time by continual and consistent glimpses, we are changed from "glory to glory." This is the created order and design of God., and I can hear Him saying, "you find Me and I'll show you who you are!" (see 2 Corinthians 3:18).

> *"My son, if you accept my words and store up my commands within you, turning your ear to wisdom and applying your heart to understanding—indeed, if you call out for insight and cry aloud for understanding, and if you look for it as for silver and search for it as for hidden treasure, then you will understand the fear of the Lord and find the knowledge of God."*
>
> – Proverbs 2:1-5 (NIV)

So the cycle continues, for the more clearly we see our destiny, the more clearly we manifest God's purposes in the earth. From this place, it's about laboring from our destination, instead of working towards it. Many believers are trying to get into the promise land, when through His Son, He has already brought us in and is calling us to operate from it. We must see ourself standing in the promise land, declaring into the fields, that this is the day of restoration. I call this "praying with an ascended lens," meaning we must see (everything including ourselves) through the eyes of heaven. We must see different in order to walk in a different realm of authority. We must see things the way Abba does. When we pray this way, we put a bold punctuation on the purposes of God and remind the enemy of his demise. As we pray with this holy perspective, it reminds him of the risen Christ - a King who manifests victory through His people. At this point, our prayers serve warning to the enemy's camp, that there is a King on the other side of the prayers and proclamations, who is ready to wage war on anything that hinders His will from going forth. As we pray with the perspective

> As we pray the ascended way, we serve vengeance on the devil's kingdom.

of heaven, the ascended way, we serve vengeance on the devil's kingdom. It's always easier to defeat your enemies when you are soaring above them.

Heaven moves and hell shakes by the power of "ascended prayer." Paul said "our struggle is not against flesh and blood, but against the rulers, against the authorities, against the powers of this dark world and against the spiritual forces of evil in the heavenly realms." (Ephesians 6:12) He's saying, "Get your eyes up where you belong and begin to war from that place!" Paul spent much of his efforts establishing the church in identity, wanting to connect the "pray without ceasing" mandate to the ascended reality, yielding a church that operated in authority and power. He envisioned intercessors and ambassadors who warred from the victory already wrought in Christ.

When the sons and daughters of God see their destiny as a peculiar people set apart to do the works of God, we begin to pray downward as partners (from the ascended view) rather than praying up as peasants (the servant view). The apostle Peter says, we are "a chosen generation, royal priesthood, a holy nation, His own special people, that you may proclaim that praises of Him who called you." (1 Peter 2:9) This is a present reality, hence "we are." The word for proclaim (in the Greek) means "to tell out or forth," denoting that we are a people of praise and prayer alike. As we understand our present position as chosen, royal and holy, we pray with a redeemed confidence. It's then that we will run to Him and not from Him in prayer. This is where breakthrough begins.

> *"...even when we were dead in our transgressions, made us alive together with Christ (by grace you have been saved), and raised us up with Him, and seated us with Him in the heavenly places in Christ Jesus."*
>
> *– Ephesians 2:5, 6 (NASB)*

Paul knew the key to possessing something was by realizing that we already have it. It's like when the Lord affirmed that the children of Israel had been given the land, but they actually had to possess it. (Joshua 1:11) It was theirs in the spirit, they just had to manifest it as a tangible reality. It's the same concept on this side of grace. The Lord has purchased the victory for us and now asks that we take hold of it. It's there in Christ, we just have to believe and walk in it. He doesn't just want a church full of theology, He wants a people filled with the living knowledge will of God, an intimate and experiential knowledge that manifests in signs, wonders, miracles, etc.

ABOVE THE CLOUDS

In the natural, an eagle will always take the serpent to his own realm (in the air) to destroy it. The reason the eagle does this, is to take the snake out of its familiar area (place of influence) and into the eagle's own domain to disorient and confuse the serpent (enemy). The eagle can fight in the air because it's where it belongs. It is the eagle's home and domain. Its nest and area of rest is there. The serpent's place of influence and familiar area is on the earth (in the flesh), but the eagle's domain is in the air (the heavens). Proverbs 30:19 confirms this, "The way of an eagle in the sky, the way of a serpent on a rock…" Friends, we must fight the enemy from the ascended place (that we belong), because the ascended place is where the enemy can't touch you or intercept your prayers. We are like that eagle. We are seated with Christ in heavenly places. Our domain is in the heavens. We may be standing on the earth but our place of rule and rest is in the heavens. It's time for the church to start praying like it!

> *"They will mount up with wings like eagles, they will run and not get tired, they will walk and not become weary."*
>
> — Isaiah 40:31b (NASB)

I remember the first time I flew on an airplane. We were headed to Broken Arrow, Oklahoma, to visit some lifelong friends. Although I was a bit nervous at my first time in the air, I was also very much excited to turn a 12 hour trip into a 3 hour one. Soon after we left the ground (and I overcame my fear of takeoff), I was amazed at how small everything below us was. I remember thinking, "The perspective up here is so much different than when you're on the ground." I pretty much forgot about everything that was going on "down there." I just got caught up in the beautiful panorama view of the earth below. The higher we got, the more amazed I was at just how small everything seemed and how beautiful the landscape was. I could see so much more from the aerial view on that jet airplane. Entire lakes, ponds, hills, and valleys were visible up there. Whereas I could only see a few feet around me on the ground, now I could see for miles and miles. It wasn't that my eyesight improved, but rather that I had a different perspective. I was seeing from an ascended view. You could say that my vision had enlarged.

Now we all know that nothing changed in the natural. The hills didn't shrink, nor did the lakes dry up. Everything was in the same state as when I was on the ground. But one thing was certain. My perspective had changed. And when my perspective changed, so did my mindset.

And this is what I'm talking about when I say ascended view. It's the perspective according to God's. It's how God sees things and is synonymous with walking or seeing in the Spirit. For when we operate in the Spirit, we are viewing things the way heaven does. I highly doubt that the God of the universe is pacing the floor of heaven, fretting over the economic status of the earth. He's in no way scurrying around trying to figure out what He's going to do with mankind's rebellion. Friends, Scripture tells us that He is seated in heaven and is at full rest. Psalm 2 says "He who sits in the heavens laughs." When chaos and calamity break out, He's got a grin on His face, not because He doesn't care but simply because He's not worried about any of its outcome. He has it all under control.

Jesus exemplified the ascended lifestyle. He lived from the throne room. Although His feet were on the earth, His vision was in heaven. God's Son was led by what He saw in heaven. He says in John 5:19, "The Son can do nothing by himself. He does only what he sees the Father doing. Whatever the Father does, the Son also does." This is why Jesus could walk on the earth and remain unshaken. Receiving ridicule after ridicule, the Son of Man could stay the course. He saw life from the Father's view.

When we pray from above, the things that once bothered us really don't bother us anymore. A thousand issues lose their influence when we get our minds (affections) on things above. It's time that we stop doing our worry any favors and lay siege on the things that hold us bound. Fear and its friends (anxiety and stress) can't live in an environment of faith and the presence of God. The very awareness of God and our calling in Him run those things out of town.

In Philippians, Paul urges the church to pray with thanksgiving and to leave the the anxiety in the dust.

> *"Be anxious for nothing, but in everything by prayer and supplication with thanksgiving let your requests be made known to God. And the peace of God, which surpasses all comprehension, will guard your hearts and your minds in Christ Jesus."*
>
> – Philippians 4:6, 7 (NASB)

Paul is urging the church to gain a different perspective in their prayer life. He's encouraging them to mix thanksgiving into the equation - to view life and its cares from a different angle. Thanksgiving is not being naive of life's issues or weights, but rather it's about seeing things differently. It's about having a different perspective. As we remain thankful, peace will soon follow.

Growing up, my family traveled to many different gatherings and various churches, so I heard many different styles of prayer. I was part of some amazing services that I wish could have continued for days, yet I sat through some that I wish would have never even begun. In some of these services, I heard many sincere Christians pray. I heard some powerful prayers and I heard some weak ones. In some cases, I heard many saints pray like peasants instead of princes - like slaves instead of saints. In particular, I remember hearing phrases like "We're just ole sinners Lord," and "Lord, have mercy for we are but filthy rags," so on and so forth. These prayers were a few revelations shy of sonship. As I realized later in life, these prayers and perspectives were intertwined with shame and a wrong view of grace. Although I grew up in a home that didn't pray like this, I soon began to think "If this is what it means to pray, no thank you!" Seriously, this is true! I assume this is why for the early part of my life, I had a disconnect with prayer and viewed it as a drudgery instead of a joy.

However, as I began to actually step into prayer for myself, I soon learned otherwise. By Holy Spirit revelation, I began to view prayer as it was - a way to partner with God in conversation. I quickly saw that it was nothing about running our nature through the mud, rather it was about standing before Him as one clean in Christ. No longer did I see myself as a filthy sinner, but as an accepted son before my heavenly Father. This reality soon began to change the way I prayed, and I no longer saw myself as a victim to sin, but rather a victor in righteousness, and my prayer life began to soar. I began to view myself right there in the throne room with Christ, praying as a king and priest that had been raised up. Friends, this is the believer's place!

It's true that we will never develop an intimate or lasting relationship with anyone who shuns us. Never will we be inclined to develop dialogue with someone who thinks we are a slob, or if they're totally disgusted with us. In fact, too many sincere believers in the body have a view of the Father according to their earthly relationships. Sadly, a generation who's been scarred in earthly relationships is usually one driven away from the Lord. This is why we need to have a right view of the Father and our place with Him in heaven, because the more we understand the knowledge of God and our identity, we will actually talk to Him more. As we see that He delights in us as His children, we will want to run to Him in prayer.

It's also crucial to understand that God wants partners, not peasants. He wants vessels He can pray and work through. John 15:15 declares, "No longer do I call you slaves, for the slave does not know what his master is doing; but I have called you friends, for all things that I have heard from My Father I have made known to you." It's amazing that He's never too busy for friendship. Rather, He boldly calls us friends. He knew what He was signing up for when He sent His Son to the earth. He desired friends who would abide in Him - those who make Him their shelter.

He wants friends who know His heart and release it in prayer.

> *"Abide in Me, and I in you. As the branch cannot bear fruit of itself unless it abides in the vine, so neither can you unless you abide in Me. I am the vine, you are the branches; he who abides in Me and I in him, he bears much fruit, for apart from Me you can do nothing."*
>
> – John 15:4, 5 (NASB)

Conversation with God is where abiding begins. It's the core activity of remaining in Christ. It's one of the most practical ways to actively engage and abide in Christ and His invitation into friendship. As we develop a lifestyle of prayer, we are reminded of His goodness and affirmed in our identity via the place of prayer. In addition, we cultivate life in God as we talk with Him. Being intentional in this way keeps our hearts alive.

As we engage with God in prayer, we begin to experience the real joy and power of prayer. He has picked you to partner with. As a child of God, you have been chosen to partner with Him to bring His Kingdom to earth. If you have given your heart to Jesus, you're not a servant, you're a saint. You are a co-heir with Christ and He wants to share His glory!

> *"The Spirit Himself testifies with our spirit that we are God's children. Now if we are children, then we are heirs—heirs of God and co-heirs with Christ, if indeed we share in His sufferings in order that we may also share in His glory."*
>
> *— Romans 8:16, 17*

ABIDING IN THE VINE

In John 15, Jesus is teaching the disciples that He is the true vine - the One sent from the Father to bring (zoe) life to the branch, to you and me. The branch had been defiled by her mingling with other "vinedressers," and she (the people of God) had given herself to the care of others. Jeremiah says of the nation of Israel, "Yet I planted you a choice vine, a completely faithful seed. How then have you turned yourself before Me into the degenerate shoots of a foreign vine?" (Jeremiah 2:21) The Message translation says it this way:

> *"You were a select vine when I planted you from completely reliable stock. And look how you've turned out - a tangle of rancid growth, a poor excuse for a vine."*

So, Jesus comes to redeem a people and install them into a Kingdom whose vinedresser is the Father. He's a King who cares. It's important to understand the culture in which Jesus was talking about. He was a Jew addressing Jews and He was speaking in a way that they would understand. So to relate His point, He uses some main terms that we must pay attention to - vine, vinedresser, branch, abide.

To tie all these points and terms together, Jesus introduces a profound concept - that we can ask anything that is in alignment with the vine, and it will be done. He says "If you abide in Me, and My words abide in you, ask whatever you wish (desire), and it will be done for you." (John 15:7) Here, Jesus was teaching us a new paradigm of prayer. You see, in the Old Testament, God didn't live inside of man. He only rested upon certain individuals such as prophets or men / women of God who were chosen for a particular time. Thus, intimacy was limited and man was always "on edge" concerning the glory and righteousness of God. It was only so close that one could get to His presence. However, Jesus comes along with this new idea that He would dwell inside of man, and man would dwell inside of Him.

This "ask whatever you wish" paradigm that Jesus is speaking about, is prayer born out of desire. It's heartfelt and fervent prayer. In Psalms 37:4, the writer says "Delight yourself in the Lord and He will give (plant in) you the desires of your heart." I've heard it preached that if we like God, he'll give us the things we've always wanted (nice car, big house, pay raise, etc…). Although those things are okay to have as long as they don't have us, it's not exactly what the Scripture is saying. The Psalmist in chapter 37 is saying, "If you will become preoccupied with God (His heart, desires, and what pleases Him), He will plant inside of you what He wants to see come forth. This usually means that He will fill your heart with such delight so that the "bigger and better stuff" loses it's primary influence. As this happens, we will find ourselves asking for different things. Instead of being consumed by our "four and no more," we become burdened for our city. We will begin to weep over souls rather than our own circumstances. We start gaining a heart to pray and seek Him more, rather than pursuing our own fleshly desires. At this point, His desires just seem to work out all the unnecessary things.

So, when we abide in Him by continual conversation, His desires become more and more clear. He's simply given us those desires that we can in turn say them back to Him. He loves to answer His own desires! We see this is the life of Solomon, when he takes over his father, David's throne. What favor there was on this young man. Solomon had received a rich heritage of pursuing the things of God. His father was the man after God's heart! (Acts 13:22) In 2 Chronicles 1, the Lord visits him in a dream and tells Him to ask for whatever he wishes. He could have asked for riches and received them. He could have petitioned heaven for all the resources allowed to be given a man, and he would have received them. The Lord is standing before Solomon with arms wide-open, daring him to just ask. Solomon, in his sincerity, asked for wisdom. Out of all the things that he could have requested, he asked for wisdom! Why? I believe it was because this young king was actually voicing the desire of the Lord. His request was mirroring God's.

In John 15, Jesus was saying "If you will just abide, remain, and stay connected to me, you will have a prayer life that sees lasting results. Born out of intimacy and desire, you will ask whatever you wish and I will answer with fruit." He calls it "fruit that remains." (John 15:16) This means that the fruit I bear from abiding, will be passed on down to my children and their children. This is good news. I don't have to struggle and strive to produce fruit; all I must do is just rest and abide in Him. This is "abiding and asking."

One of the important truths that Jesus declares is that Abba, our heavenly Father, is a vinedresser. I'm sure when He said this, the disciples' ears perked up. What's important about this is a vinedresser was very involved in the process of the vine. Vinedressers (who is also called a "husbandman") weren't merely farmers or gardeners, but were professionals in taking care of plants. The dressers' function was to nurture, prune, and provide everything needed to raise it, that it may produce lasting and healthy fruit. They were very committed to raising up good vines (vineyards) and understood that they would have to care for their vines for years. Unlike many plants we know of today, vines would live for decades. Webster calls a vinedresser as a "specialist in the area of farming." This is what Jesus was saying about His Father, that He was a professional when it comes to caring for the vine, His church. He loves being involved in the care, the pruning, and most of all seeing the fruit that it bears.

Aren't you glad that our vinedresser (Abba Father) doesn't treat us like an old weed, but pays attention with such detail. He's not interested in using a "crop duster" to nurture us, but He walks among us and cares for us intimately. Revelation tells us that the Son (who is the express desire of the Father), walks among the lamp stand, His church. (Revelation 1:12-13) He doesn't just pat us on the head and wish us luck, rather, He cares for each one of us with such intricate detail. He knows the number of hairs on our head and His thoughts towards us are as numerous as the sands of the sea. (Psalm 139:18) He is a good Father and vinedresser!

So, He says that anyone who gives home to His Word, would be able to access anything he wants by simply asking. I understand there is the constraint of time on every prayer, but to know that when we utter desires from the place of abiding in Him, He will answer us somehow and some way. It's His promise. Again, He loves to answer His own desires from the cry of His people. Therefore, the degree that we talk to the Spirit is the degree that we walk in the Spirit.

four

The Secret Place

If one must be violent, let him be violent about guarding his heart before The Lord. Be violent in cultivating the secret place. Forgive. Love. Press into God. Don't lose the secret place.

What an amazing time to be alive! It seems that there is so much Holy Spirit activity across the earth - from the mission fields in Asia to the prayer rooms of this nation, from evangelism in the villages of Africa to the intercession rising out of Israel, God is definitely moving. It's exciting! With all this activity, I believe it's crucial that we run into the secret place, into the place of encounter. The Holy Spirit wants us to live from the fountainhead of intimacy and encounter. He's calling us away to touch our hearts that we may touch the nations. It's evident throughout Scripture, that He always first encounters a man before He does a nation.

The desire to commune with man is an ancient truth in the heart of God. He just loves fellowship with man. From the roots of Genesis to His return in Revelation, God has been fighting to get back onto the scene - to be deeply involved in the affairs of men. He wants to restore them to Eden reality, where He encounters His people and releases His dominion. He declared this mission in Exodus 25:8 when He told Moses, "Let them construct a sanctuary for Me, that I may dwell among them." The Hebrew word for dwell is shakan, meaning "to settle down, abide, reside." Another definition is "tabernacle," and is where we get the phrase "tabernacle of Moses." Yahweh Himself was calling a nation to build a place (set apart with the attributes of Eden), that He could sit down in the midst of His people. This yearning inside God's heart could no longer only be kept reserved for His angels, but had to be shared with mankind. God was most interested in getting involved in the affairs of men. He wanted to draw close and have conversation with His creation.

> "The greatest secret is the secret place."
>
> – Bob Sorge

ENCOUNTERING HIS LONGING

Out of God's burning desire to dwell with man, we as believers (who were made in His image) possess the same yearning and innate desire to dwell with Him. I guess you could say that encounter is in our DNA. Therefore, understanding the truth that God yearns for the nearness of His people is crucial for growing in prayer. When David said "zeal for Your house has consumed me" (Psalm 69:9), it was only a direct reflection of God's fiery zeal for David. It wasn't that the young king had obtained this zeal by his own discipline or strength or that he had learned it at the latest conference. Rather, David had come into contact with the fiery heart of God. This young man experienced a head-on collision with the love that burns in the heart of God, and he began to manifest it in the natural. This was David's secret. He was able to connect with the Lord's affections. He was able to break past the immediate pressure and see the Lord's longing and delight for him. His heart was trained in going after God's. David had a PhD in the pursuit of God.

> *"He led me to a place of safety;*
> *He rescued me because He delights in me."*
>
> *— Psalm 18:19 (NLT)*

One morning while in prayer, the Lord suddenly swept over me with a wave of His love. To be honest, I wasn't expecting it. I was just doing my usual devotion time and He totally surprised me! It's like He walked into the room and I could feel the tangible weight of His presence. I had only experienced this type of encounter one other time in my life. Honestly, I usually don't experience dramatic times like this, but usually more subtle touches. Nevertheless, there was something major going on in this moment. As I experienced the weight of His presence, I fell to the floor on my knees, pressing my face to the ground. It was such a powerful moment. It's amazing that such a gentle love can have such a reverential fear attached to it. His love is tender yet tenacious. Undone by His presence, I began to sense the Lord singing over me. I could feel the heat of His gaze as He ministered to me. It felt like He was standing over top of me and singing His song of love. I kept hearing "Robby, it's all about love and this love is a Man. It's Me." As soon as He said this, I began to weep profusely. I entered into a new dimension of understanding this Man

- His heart of tenderness but also His powerful presence. Hearing this, I just continued to go deeper into worship. I had encountered more than an abstraction; I encountered a Person. From this day forward, I have never been the same, especially related to the love of God. I feel that this encounter was an "upgrade," one that touched and will continue to touch every part of my life. Experiencing His love has transformed me into a "new man."

The Apostle John said it like this, "we love because He first loved us" (1 John 4:19). John, being another expert in the love of God, writes the key ingredient to experiencing the love of almighty God - it was in seeing His love for us. Keep in mind, John was the one who writes of his extravagant love for Jesus. He was an enthusiastic lover of God, calling himself the "one whom Jesus loved" (John 13:23). not in a negative prideful kind of way, but in a childlike fashion. The Greek word for "love" here is "agapao" meaning "loved dearly, to be well pleased". It denotes a special kind of favored love. It's the "over-the-top" love. In this verse, it seems that John was boasting of God's love for him. It looks as if he's saying, "I know Jesus loved all His disciples, but really, Jesus was crazy about me." This was just the excited view of Jesus' love. He felt that he was God's favorite, simply because the Lord has a way of doing that to His children. He singles in on the individual with such intensity that you feel that you're the only one in the room. The heat of His gaze builds one up in amazing ways. John was eager to make this known.

I can just imagine the look on the other disciples' faces as they read John's account of the gospel. They're really liking the whole "God in flesh" thing, and how John writes of Jesus' humanity and deity.

But things change in chapter 13. John begins to boast of Jesus' love for him. I can see them saying, "did John just bring special attention to Jesus' love for him? Hey, who is this guy boasting of God's love for him. The audacity! The nerve to say that Jesus possessed a special kind of love for him!" I agree that this phrase is a bit bold, but it shows John's eagerness of the disciple in God's love. As some would say, he was a bit "giddy."

John was a man who defined his success in lying on God's heart and receiving His love. He was the disciple who reclined on the heart of Jesus at the last supper (John 13:25). Such an act was considered by the Jews a mark of special honor and favor for one to be permitted to lie in the bosom of the master of the feast. Friends, the ability to love God and receive the love of God is paramount to any ministry success or accomplishment. It is one of the marks of highest favor and honor in the Kingdom. Living in the love of God is the goal! It's the place of ultimate rest, joy, and peace.

The apostle and beloved disciple was saying that the source of all zeal, passion, and holy desire (affection) comes straight from the heart of our Creator. The created can't find the remedies of life in itself. We must seek the source and provider. We must live in pursuit of the Creator, for this is the means to an end and the end itself. Perhaps the reason John received the greatest revelation of end-time prophecy was due to the fact that he stewarded the love of God unlike any other. His worshiping heart ushered his eyes to see what the angels saw.

It's in prayer that we are connected to this reality. Prayer gives us momentary glimpses of the closeness and nearness of God. When we sit down and slow down long enough, He will remind our hearts of His burning desire to bring us close. It's in prayer that we ask for multiplied revelation and it's in prayer that we often encounter it. Adam walked in the cool of the day with God, and every time that I surrender my busy schedule to conversation with God, my heart is calibrated to enjoy the cool of that revelation.

OUT OF THE SHADE AND INTO THE SHADOW

Several times in Scripture it talks about the word "shadow." It is often associated with "wings" and denotes "covering or protection." Just like we seek shelter in the shadow from the scorching heat, so Scripture encourages us to do the same - seek shelter from the scorching accusations and lies of the enemy. The meaning paints the picture of a baby chick who would seek protection and covering of the momma hen. Protection and covering is at the heart of His presence. David said "For in the day of trouble He will conceal me in His tabernacle; in the secret place of His tent He will hide me; He will lift me up on a rock". (Psalm 27:5) With it's meaning, it has a main two fold application - the shadow of death (enemy and evil) and the shadow of the Lord, which is life and peace. The contrast is seen all throughout Scripture (see Psalm 23:4 and 57:1). One we are to seek shelter away from and the other we are to seek shelter into.

Moses says in Psalm 91 "He who dwells in the shelter (secret place) of the Most High, will abide in the shadow of the Almighty." David cried out "keep me as the apple of your eye; hide me in the shadow of Your wings" (Psalm 17:8), and again declares in Psalm 36:7, "How precious is Your lovingkindness, O God! And the children of men who take refuge in the shadow of Your wings."   Two of the most powerful men of God in Scripture declare the reality of God's protection of His shadow. I believe the place of hiding and refuge was their favorite place in God. They loved the secret place! Seeking and running into God's shadow isn't a sign of weakness, but rather a sign of great strength, wisdom, and faith in the Lord.

> *"One thing I have desired of the Lord, that will I seek… to inquire in His temple."*
>
> — Psalm 27:4

The Lord spoke to me one morning in my quiet time and said, "It's time to get out of the shade and into the shadow." He sometimes speaks to me in these types of wise and clever phrases - not audibly, just by little impressions and thoughts. When I first heard Him say it this way, I was a bit confused and decided to lean in a little. After an hour or so of pondering what He had said, I began to understand that the shade He was speaking of alluded to the "comforts of life". Things that we hold so dearly but at times steal our affection for Him. It may be television, media, music, or simply just too much "good stuff." It's whatever comfort that keeps you in "lounging" mode. I'm not talking about (Biblical) rest, I'm talking about the lazy approach to God, the mode that causes our heart to disengage and lose focus. The approach that lacks urgency. In essence, He was declaring that it's time to get out of the shade of the comforts of life, and into the shadow of His presence (protection, the secret place of His dwelling)".

David said it this way - "Surely I will not enter my house, Nor lie on my bed; I will not give sleep to my eyes or slumber to my eyelids, until I find a place for the Lord, a dwelling place for the Mighty One

> *If we want to enjoy the benefits of the secret place, the place of hiding under His protection, we must war anything that opposes that.*

of Jacob" (Psalm 132:3-5). The writer says of David in verse one, "Remember O Lord, on David's behalf, all his affliction; how he swore to the Lord and vowed to the Mighty One." King David was being remembered for his vow to build God a dwelling place, and in turn to provide a shadow for God's people in the land. He wanted to stay covered and protected by the Lord's shadow during his reign, shedding his life of any "shade" that would lure him into "lounging mode." Rather, he desired to stay in "presence mode" and introduce a whole nation to it. As we see in his language throughout the Psalms, any other "covering" was not an option for this young man. If it meant embracing affliction (of going against the grain of the age) to enjoy the shadow and presence of God in Jerusalem, that's just what it was going to be. He understood that hosting God's presence meant paying a price.

> *"We sacrifice for what satisfies. The soul-satisfying riches in the presence of God propel us out of our comfort zones, calling us out of the warm confines of our beds to our knees in early-morning prayer and meditation on God's word."*
>
> – *God Dwells Among Us* by G.K. Beale and Mitchell Kim

The first part of 2016, we experienced a huge snowstorm that kept us inside for a couple of days. It was showing no signs of letting up, so we decided to "purge" and clean our house, and according to my lovely bride, I was responsible for cleaning my office. It had been a long time coming and boy, did I dread it. But to have a clean office and a happy wife, it had to be worth it! So, I jumped in with both feet and discovered things I didn't know I had. I found year-old coupons, expired receipts, ancient documents, old pictures, and even an autographed CD from a great worship leader friend. After aggravated allergies and what seemed like an entire day, I felt like I had a new office. It even smelled better. I had allowed so much debris to pile up over time, that I didn't even realize it until I stood in the middle of my clean office. We must be intentional about keeping our time and schedules free of clutter. Over time, things can pile up and get out of hand. Whatever it is, we must intentionally keep our "offices" clean and free of clutter. The reward is a renewed confidence and fresh awareness.

NOISE - THE GREAT ENEMY

In an age of many options, I believe one the greatest challenges is slowing down. The great enemy of the hour is simply noise. With everything at our finger tips and every form of communication being made more accessible, it is the struggle of every man and woman to find quality and quiet time. I've heard it (busyness) called "satan's favorite tactic." The question of this generation is not "can we find something to do," but rather "can we find someone doing the one thing?" In this age, there is so much to do, so much to see, and so many needs to tend to. However, the real question is, "Who will stay focused and intent on the very thing that's on His heart?" In the busyness of life, who will embrace the secret place?

We see many Biblical examples of men and women of God encountering "noise" as they pursued the Lord. From Genesis to Revelation, the heroes of the faith were those who tuned out the noise and pressed through for the glory of their God. The noise varied from satan's accusations to their own weaknesses, and though they weren't perfect, their faith was proven by a diligent pursuit (Hebrews 11).

One of the leading Biblical examples (of tuning out the noise) is in the story of Mary of Bethany. It's one of the few stories whose account is presented in all four gospels (Matthew 26:6-13; Mark 14:3-9; Luke 7:36-50; John 12:1-8). It's a very important story and one to pay attention to. In it, we find this young lady Mary coming into the house of Simon simply because she heard that Jesus was there. We see that His presence demanded hers. As she walks into the scene with the Pharisees and Jesus' elite twelve, she goes right up to the King of glory. She wastes no time in her pursuit, but enters with one thing in mind - to worship and adore the One whom her soul loves. Her worship was focused. She didn't come empty handed, but gladly brought a gift and offering - ointment purchased with her earnings, possibly even a year's wage. As you read this story, remind yourself that worship demands an offering, and often times a costly one.

As Mary of Bethany encounters the Man from Nazareth, Luke tells us "standing behind Him at His feet, weeping, she began to wet His feet with her tears, and kept wiping them with the hair of her head, and kissing His feet and anointing them with the perfume" (Luke 7:38). It's obvious that this young lady was fascinated with the glory of this Man, and she was there to express it. With no regard to her surroundings, she isolates her focus on the very object of worship. On display for all to see, she's responding to the King of kings with outlandish worship. What is happening here..? What's causing this one to give what she had?

The thing that Jesus delighted in was not just the offering of her ointment. It wasn't just the tears that she cried or the expression (sound or style) of her worship. Jesus was captured by her heart to worship. Yahweh has always had a soft spot for worshippers. He absolutely adores a worshiping heart.

> *"The Lord said to Samuel, do not consider his appearance or his height, for I have rejected him. The Lord does not look at the things people look at. People look at the outward appearance, but the Lord looks at the heart."*
>
> *– 1 Samuel 16:7*

This young lady from Bethany found Him worthy enough to tune out the noise of her accusers and press into the moment of adoring the one whom she loved. This is the glory of the secret place.

> *Jesus was captured by her heart to worship - Yahweh has always had a soft spot for worshippers.*

When no one else is looking or is even around, we set ourselves apart as the offering, so that our lives may ascend to His throne. It's one thing to bring an offering and another to actually become the offering. This is why Paul said in Romans 12:1, "Therefore, I urge you, brothers and sisters, in view of God's mercy, to offer your bodies as a living sacrifice, holy and pleasing to God–this is your true and proper worship" (NIV). Paul paints a glorious picture of worship in this passage, one where we worship by bringing our lives as the pleasing sacrifice. You don't have to be a musician, singer, a preacher, or prophet to worship. You don't need a pulpit or even a pew. All you need is a yielded heart. We see that Mary of Bethany changed history because she became the offering.

Her life and heart became the fragrance of incense before the Son of God. It didn't matter who was around or who was looking in, she was going to pour out her ointment as an act of love and simplistic devotion to the Man who could give her eternal purpose and destiny.

We see that Jesus responds to Mary and says of the moment, "In pouring this ointment on my body, she has done it to prepare me for burial. Truly I say to you, wherever this gospel is proclaimed in the whole world, what she has done will also be told in memory of her" (Matthew 26:12-13). This extravagant act of worship has become one of the Bible's defining love stories. It has been preserved in the Scripture to provoke generations who follow, to just simply pour it all out and sit at His feet. This eternal act of worship would ring through the halls of history, urging generations to choose the one thing, the secret place.

ONE THING IS NEEDED

"But one thing is needed, and Mary has chosen that good part, which will not be taken away from her."

– Luke 10:42

In the rush and mundanity of every day life, we must press pass the noise of today and seek to be that kind of worshipper who regards nothing but the very object of worship - this Man from Nazareth. As you read this story, ask yourself, is my life one full of noise? I'm not talking about loud and boisterous praise. We want that. We need to be a people of exuberant and lively praise. What I'm referring to is the noise of distraction, to where your heart is divided and given to lesser pleasures. It's the noise that leads to a distorted view of His love and ultimately leads us into boredom. I'm not only associating it with volume or amplitude, but the amount of traffic (activity) we have going on. This is why we can be in a quiet room with no obvious distractions, yet still be battling to quiet our hearts and minds before the Lord. Quietness is as much a condition of the heart as it is an outward expression of the body.

Ask the Lord for grace to press past the noise and "urgency" of today and press into the secret place. For some, it may be starting the day out with a quiet time before the Lord. For others it may be before you go to bed. Whatever time of day and setting, He wants the secret place in your life more than you want it. The Lord is eager to hide you in the shadow of His wings. He's been there and understands the demands and pressures of the day. He desires to break us out of the jail cell of boredom and make us a secret place people.

> *"One of the most counter-cultural things you can do is sit down, be quiet, and listen."*
>
> – Cory Russell

TOO BUSY TO PRAY OR TOO BUSY NOT TO PRAY?

> *"I have so much to do that I shall spend the first three hours in prayer."*
>
> – Martin Luther

It was a Friday morning and I had a long day ahead of me. I needed to finish my Sunday sermon, make the weekly newsletter, sit down with some colleagues, meet an electrician, edit the ministry website, and the list goes on and on. It was a "loaded legal pad" kind of day. One of those where lunch was more than likely not going to happen. As I looked over my day, I quickly became very overwhelmed. I thought, "How did my schedule get so full?" Thoughts of anxiety and stress soon flooded my mind and I had no idea where I was even going to begin. With nearly more things on my to-do list than hours in my work day, how was I going to meet the deadlines and pressures? Thankfully, I decided I wasn't going to. Instead, I moved a few things around, postponed a couple of meetings, and I simply "turned off the noise." There were good things that I was doing, but at the time, it was making for a crowded and noisy day and it wasn't what the Lord had for me at the time. You see, there are times when you will be very active in ministry and that's fine as long as He's in it. However, if He's not, then friends, it is nothing but noise. It actually becomes the very thing that will choke out His voice in your life (Mark 4:19). He will never stop speaking. It's just that you'll stop hearing.

Unfortunately, I have been in this situation way too many times, where I've piled the things on. And maybe you're nodding your head agreeing with me here. The sad fact is, too many of us are way too busy. Our planners are full while often our hearts are empty. The to-do lists are covered with chores, yet the time to connect with anyone is just out of the picture. Friends, this is not good!

One may say that they are too busy to pray, but I believe we're too busy not to pray. With so many things swirling through our minds and our hearts, I would assume that it's borderline insane that we would even consider not living a life of prayer. Sounds a bit aggressive I know, but I have learned this the hard way. In fact, in my own personal experience, the busy "rat race" has been the greatest hinderance to developing a life of prayer. It's something I war with constantly. Sometimes my most anointed times in ministry are when I learned to say "NO" to the things that were pulling me away from the secret place.

> *"Self control is not the ability to say no to a bunch of things. It is the ability to say yes to one thing!"*
>
> *– Danny Silk*

Jesus modeled this better than any one. This young man from Nazareth had more demands on His ministry than any of His contemporaries, and it would be safe to say that He had (many) more demands than any of us do some 2,000 years later. In fact, many times we see that the demands on His ministry were almost unbearable. He was doing the works of the kingdom and it was attractive to the masses. He was casting out devils, opening the blind eyes, causing the dumb to speak, among many other miracles. Several times the gospels record that He healed "all" disease and sickness (Matthew 4:23; 9:35; Luke 4:40). Often times He would do 100% miracles. Not half, not even 9 out of 10… 100%! This is enough to draw a crowd!

We also see on a couple occasions, that He fed thousands of people on a sack lunch. This type of "multiplication" ministry is going to attract the masses. When you're multiplying everything that your hands touch, talk about gaining "ministry momentum." John 6:2 says, "A large crowd followed Him, because they saw the signs which He was performing on those who were sick." Mark accounts,

"Jesus could no longer publicly enter a city, but stayed out in unpopulated areas; and they were coming to Him from everywhere" (Mark 1:45). Simply put, Jesus' ministry was exploding. They were coming from everywhere - from Samaria, Capernaum, Galilee... everywhere! Jesus was truly becoming the Great Physician for many cities and areas.

> *"The news about Him spread throughout all Syria; and they brought to Him all who were ill, those suffering with various diseases and pains, demoniacs, epileptics, paralytics; and He healed them. Large crowds followed Him from Galilee and the Decapolis and Jerusalem and Judea and from beyond the Jordan"*
>
> *– Matthew 4:24, 25*

In light of this, we see that Jesus remained steady in living a life of prayer. He knew the demands on His life and ministry, and knew that He must stay engaged with what the Father was saying and doing. In His physical limitations, He realized the demands required close communion with Abba. "Truly, truly, I say to you, the Son can do nothing of Himself, unless it is something He sees the Father doing; for whatever the Father does, these things the Son also does in like manner" (John 5:19).

Mark says of Jesus' secret place, "In the early morning, while it was still dark, Jesus got up, left the house, and went away to a secluded place, and was praying there" (Mark 1:35). Jesus awoke the dawn with a heart ready to encounter His Father. He rose up early to run into the secret place. He went from the multitudes to the mountains. It was on the mountain that He received strength and perspective for the multitudes. If I've learned one thing about being a minister of the gospel, this would be it: You can't give from what you don't have. It's almost ridiculous to think that we can. As ridiculous, is saying that we can draw water from a dry well. It just isn't going to happen.

Being fully man, Jesus kept His heart engaged with the Father by conversation and communion in prayer. He had experienced the rest of His Father in the secret place. Consequently, He could say, "come unto me you who are weary and heavy laden." As a man surrounded by the limitations of time and space, Jesus found it paramount to invest in the secret place. He went away into the still and secluded place to hear what the Father would say to Him. This is why the disciples would urge Him to teach them to pray. It was actually out of the place of prayer that Jesus came walking on the water and wowing His disciples. "After He had sent the crowds away, He went up on the mountain by Himself to pray; and when it was evening, He was there alone" (Matthew 14:23). Perhaps Jesus could see the battered boat from the ascended place.

> *Jesus awoke the dawn with a heart ready to encounter His Father. He rose up early to run into the secret place. He went from the multitudes to the mountains.*

Jesus gave us an example of what redeemed humans can accomplish by being filled with the Spirit. His life taught us how to pray. You may not have the same luxuries of praying alone as does a "full-time minister" or a single person. You may be working 60 hours a week, raising 5 kids, and have heightened demands on your life. You may be so covered up with responsibility that you can hardly see straight. Or you may have plenty of room on your schedule and are looking for a wise investment of your time. Well, for all cases, look no further. Whether you can give 10 minutes or 2 hours a day to the secret place, I encourage you to start somewhere. Give what you have and ask the Holy Spirit to breathe on it. Remember, it's not about the amount necessarily as much as it is about the stewardship. If you're doing your best with the 15 minutes you have and you possess the heart to grow in intimacy with Jesus, then you are just as good as the one who prays 1 hour a day and is content with staying where he is. Steward what you have with excellence and then ask Him for more. Both postures are breeding grounds for increase.

THE SECRET OF THE MAN AFTER GOD'S OWN HEART

David expresses his passion for the secret place in the "one thing" Psalm (Psalm 27). In one of the most quoted passages in Scripture, he begins the chapter by saying, "The Lord is my light and my salvation, so why should I be afraid? The Lord is my fortress, protecting me from danger, so why should I tremble?" He then proceeds to declare the enemies of his soul and his kingdom. The enemies of fear and dread encamp against him. Keep in mind that Psalm 27 is mostly about war and enemy threats. After spending three verses on this, he drops a bomb in the reader's lap. It's almost like David is bringing this whole idea to a crescendo, only to hit home his idea. In the suspense of danger and fear, the man after God's own heart says this most defining statement - "One thing I have asked from the Lord, that I shall seek; that I may dwell in the house of the Lord all the days of my life, to behold the beauty of the Lord and to meditate in His temple" (Psalm 27:4).

Just verses later, David declares "For in the day of trouble He will conceal me in His tabernacle; in the secret place of His tent He will hide me; He will lift me up on a rock." David's hiding place was the tabernacle (tent). It was the dwelling place of God. This was one of the main benefits of the tabernacle, that man could hide in God. To David, refuge from the enemies (of fear and dread) was right there in the tabernacle (presence) of God. It wasn't in his own home so much as it was in the house of the Lord. It wasn't at his best friend's house or the local restaurant. It was in God's dwelling place, the tabernacle. It was the place where worship ascended by creative expressions of intercession, song, dance, and music. This is why David continued to run into the house of the Lord (Psalm 69:9).

Many wanted David's throne and his widespread fame, even his own son Absalom (2 Samuel 15-19). They desired the luxury of David's kingdom. However, these men didn't possess the type of hunger that David did. Matched with the pursuit of David's outside enemies, was a man's hot pursuit of the Lord. For this young man, there was no other option. The presence of the Lord was his great escape and favorite place of retreat. The fear and danger would overwhelm him if he wouldn't choose to be overwhelmed by God's greatness. This was a choice that David made!

If this generation wants the same said of them, we must embrace the secret place - the place where no one else is around but us and Him. We must run into the secret place with wholeheartedness. It's time to shut the door, silence all distractions, and seek the greatest place in all of history - the quiet chambers of His presence. All other encounters stem from this place. As Bob Sorge says, "the greatest secret of the Kingdom is the secret place." I believe this to be true.

If the enemy can get us so "busy" and distracted from this ancient treasure of intimacy with the Lord, we will surely lose our way.

I would venture to say that once people conquer the secret place (by actually consistently and faithfully doing it), they will then begin to see a conquering in the realm of ministry. Overcoming in the private makes for overcoming in the public. Those who are bound to the Lord in the quiet will then begin to bind things in the spirit. Jesus taught us in Matthew 6, if you want to find your Father, He's behind the shut door. His reward is behind the closed quarters. He's in the secret place!

> *"But you, when you pray, go into your inner room, close your door and pray to your Father who is in secret, and your Father who sees what is done in secret will reward you."*
>
> – Matthew 6:6

NEHEMIAH - BUILDING FROM THE GROUND UP

When I think of the secret place in Scripture, I'm also reminded of the story of Nehemiah. It says early in the account, that this young man received news of his hometown being destroyed by fire and made desolate (Nehemiah 1:3). What God destined to be the great city of God's dwelling, it now was mere rubble. Upon hearing this news, he began to weep with fasting, prayer, repentance, and calling on the promises of God (1:4-11). It's evident early on, that this young man is a man of deep devotion unto the Lord. In fact, the desire that he possessed was a direct reflection of the Lord's heart for the land and people of Jerusalem. Nehemiah wept over Jerusalem because God did.

As the story unfolds, we see that Nehemiah keeps the fire burning by maintaining a prayer life. I love the phrase early on that says, "...I CONTINUED fasting and praying BEFORE the God of heaven" (1:4). First of all, "he continued" denotes that he had already established a prayer and fasting lifestyle. Secondly, he was doing it before the God of heaven, not before his friends, not even before his family. He was seeking in prayer before God. This is the core of the priestly calling, doing ministry before the audience of One. It's about standing to minister to His heart and intercede for His promises to come forth.

It's key to understand that all of Nehemiah's leadership and building were birthed out of the occurrences of chapter one and two - by seeking the Lord in wholehearted ways of prayer and fasting. We see that 8 verses (4-11) of chapter one are given to prayer. This is over half the chapter. The building that Nehemiah was doing early on was one of prayer and intercession in the secret place. He was having conversation with God before he was having it with men. Before he began erecting the wall, he first fortified his heart. This is where it all began!

By himself, Nehemiah began to cry out to the Lord in desperation. Phrases like, "let your ear be attentive and your eyes open, to hear the prayer of your servant..." (1:6) show us the desperation of Nehemiah. He eagerly desired the Lord's intervention. This young man knew if he could just get the attention of heaven, he would get the breakthrough. He knew if he could get heaven on the scene, everything else would follow. We see that Nehemiah breaks through in intercession. I see chapter one as his RESPONSE and chapter two as the Lord's REWARD. Nehemiah responds in prayer and the Lord rewards him by giving favor with the king. King Artaxerxes notices Nehemiah bearing the burden of the fallen walls and releases him to build (2:1, 2).

Nehemiah found favor with the king of Persia because He had already found it with the KING of heaven in the secret place. His pounding on the courts of heaven created a pathway for the King's courts. This remains true today. Those who want to function in effective ministry among men, must embrace the primary secret ministry with the Lord. As our hands go up in the secret place, His word will go forth (on our behalf) in the open. Jesus said it this way, "When you pray, go into your room and <u>shut the door</u> and pray to your Father who is in secret. And <u>your Father who sees in secret</u> will reward you" (Matthew 6:6).

One of the defining marks of someone who embraces and lives from the secret place is he bears the burden of the Lord. Once you get around the "Lord of the breakthrough," He begins to rub off on you. It was the Lord's burden (to redeem Jerusalem as the city of His dwelling and safety) and Nehemiah took it to the place of prayer, into the secret place. The burden that's taken up in the context of intimacy is a sure victory. His burden is light and his yoke is easy. When Jesus broke the power of sin, He gave us a garment of praise in exchange for the spirit of heaviness. He has given us the oil of gladness instead of mourning (Isaiah 61:3). Therefore, I believe intercessors should be the most joyful and happiest people on the face of the earth.

Often times our greatest breakthrough is not behind an open door, but a shut one. Warfare begins with a bended heart in the secret place. This is why we must not just focus on the pulling down of strongholds, but the bending down of the human heart. It's the bended heart that will inevitably pull down those strongholds. And there is no greater place to learn a yielded life than in the secret place. It's where the soldiers get trained. When sports teams practice, they do it behind closed doors, in private gyms, and on lonely fields. They don't sell tickets to their practices, nor do they invite the general public. Rather, they focus on what matters most by cultivating their minds and bodies for game time. The athletes present themselves before the coach and trainers to improve their level of endurance and strength, as there is constant interaction with the training staff to bring the level of play to a whole new level. The level of improvement will then be brought onto the stadiums and fields as they seek to conquer their "enemy." It's in these isolated fields of training that champions are made.

As we see through these champions of the faith, getting away to a secret and secluded place to pray and commune with God is a definite key to our growth in the Lord. It's absolutely necessary to grow in our relationship with the Holy Spirit. Those who champion the secret place will be the ones who are champions in the fields. Acts 3 (signs, wonders, acts of power) takes place with those who do Mark 9 (ascending the mountain to pray with Jesus). No man is above (or will conquer beyond) his own prayer life. May we continue embracing the secret place. He is urging His people to shut the door and open their hearts. He wants encounter in the secret place - that place where no one else is around. Beloved, He wants to tell us His secrets and unfold His mysteries. May we get away just to fellowship and commune with our Father. He is waiting there.

five
Kings & Priests

In His famous "Sermon on the Mount" (Matthew 5-7), Jesus lays out the "constitution of the Kingdom." In the 3 chapter teaching, He uses exhortations like, "worry not" and "store up treasures in heaven," asking that we pursue only a few things and warns us of things that can hinder our walk with Him, urging us to stay clear from those lesser pleasures. To conclude the exhortation of Matthew 6, He makes a most profound statement. "Seek first the kingdom of God and His righteousness…" (Matthew 6:33). I can imagine the sobriety and determination in the Lord's voice. He says, "Seek first!" - Pursue it above all other things. Go after it with wholehearted intensity and allow nothing to come in front of or take the place of it. In a few words, the Son of Man brings everything into a clear and focused perspective.

As simple as this commandment ("seek first") sounds, there is also much depth to it. The sayings of Jesus are just simply profound, meaning that one can take Jesus' words at face value and they will work, yet when you dig deeper, you will find that they have many layers of truth inside.

To be honest, I used to struggle with this passage and although I have always found inspiration in it, I couldn't fathom the thought that we were to chase down what was already in us. I didn't understand how we are supposed to seek something that we already have. We all know that the believer contains the Kingdom of God in his spirit. It's inside each believer. Jesus even states this truth in the gospel of Luke - "Now when He was asked by the Pharisees when the kingdom of God would come, He answered them and said, "The kingdom of God does not come with observation; nor will they say, 'See here!' or 'See there!' For indeed, <u>the kingdom of God is within you</u>" Luke 17:20-21 (NKJV). Jesus was stating that whenever His word and will is found at home in the believer's heart, the Kingdom of God has reign and rule. Under King Jesus' leadership, the inner chambers of this person's heart becomes a landing strip for the activity of the Spirit. This is the Kingdom of God living on the inside of every believer. In addressing the church of Corinth, Paul says that we house the very glory of God. He says "Do you not know that <u>your body is a temple of the Holy Spirit who is in you</u>, whom you have from God" (1 Cor. 6:19). In other words, we give residence to the Kingdom (Kings domain). His home finds a place of dwelling inside of ours.

It's the same with righteousness, for once we received Jesus into our heart, things drastically changed. We became the righteousness of God in Christ Jesus (2 Cor, 5:21), meaning that how the Father sees the Son, that's how He sees us. Being in Christ, I carry in my spirit the same virtue of righteousness that the Son of God does.

> *We don't get a "watered-down version" of the Holy Spirit inside of us, nor do we get a duplicate. Beloved, we get what Christ has.*

We don't get a "watered down version" of the Holy Spirit inside of us, nor do we get a duplicate. Beloved, we get what Christ has. We get His Kingdom, with all its virtues and resources. What is His is now mine. Just as a spouse gets possession of what the other has, so do I get what my beloved (Jesus) has. I am His, He is mine!

"I am my beloveds and my beloved is mine"

– Song of Songs 6:3

So again, I was confused. Why does the Son of Man urge us to pursue what is already vibrantly living on the inside of every believer? I can't imagine giving people something, then asking them to seek it out. Why should they? They already have it in their possession. However, as we all know, all of Jesus' words carry deep significance and meaning. Whatever He says at any time is designed to lead us into greater search. Always saying what the Father was saying, Jesus spoke out of the divine counsel and wisdom of God. Everything that comes from His mouth carries eternal weight and mystery. His words cannot be underestimated, only searched out for deep and lasting meaning. So, Jesus is saying something here that we must dig into.

After wrestling with this text for some time, I've discovered that He is saying something interesting here. Jesus is urging us on in our eternal calling as kings and priests. He was telling His young disciples to pursue and to "seek first" the glorious identity of kings who rule with Him and priests who minister to Him. When He said "seek first the Kingdom," He was referring to our (kingly) call in Him. When He said "seek first… righteousness," He was referring to our (priestly) call in Him. Kings represent a kingdom; Priests represent righteousness. Christ, who is both the King and Great High Priest, has restored us to the place as kings and priests, and He is urging us to go deeper in this reality, not merely as a theology, but as an experiential knowledge. In His eternal perspective, we are these things already, He just wants a people who will live embracing and digging deeper into this truth, mostly by beholding the Great High Priest. Hebrews 3:1 instructs us, "Therefore, holy brethren, partakers of a heavenly calling, consider Jesus, the Apostle and High Priest of our confession." The Greek word for "consider" is katanoeō, meaning "to perceive, observe, fix one's eyes or mind upon." This passage clearly instructs us to behold and look upon the Man Christ Jesus as the image of the perfect Priest and great Apostle, that we may become more like Him. He wants us to seek this reality out (first) because He actually wants us living from it. It's a liberating concept! He knows that once we receive and walk out our identity as kings and priests, a new confidence is released and we are positioned for victory and great breakthrough.

You see, it was in the days of Moses that God called the people of Israel to be a people set apart for His good pleasure. One of the ways that He would set them apart would be to call them into priesthood - a royal and reigning one. A priesthood who would both minister to the King and administer His Kingdom. This calling actually originated in the garden of Eden, where God called Adam (man) to walk with God and to "be fruitful and multiply" in the earth (Genesis 1:28). God would establish man to be a Kingdom of priests who bore the image of the King, releasing His reign and rule through worship and fellowship. So God calls Moses to build

His throne (dwelling place) as they established this call (Exodus 25:8). Oh the glorious reality of God's calling on the believer:

> "...you shall be to Me <u>a kingdom of priests and a holy nation</u>. These are the words that you shall speak to the sons of Israel."
>
> – Exodus 19:6

In light of the New Covenant, the Apostle Peter later affirms this calling, saying,

> "But you are a <u>chosen race, a royal priesthood, a holy nation, a people for God's own possession</u>, so that you may proclaim the excellencies of Him who has called you out of darkness into His marvelous light."
>
> – 1 Peter 2:9

As we see, the priesthood of believers is nothing new, rather it is an ancient truth. One of the primary restorations found in the death and resurrection of Jesus was the people of God entering back into their eternal destiny of priests and kings (Revelation 1:6). In the age to come, Jesus will rule over a Kingdom of priests, those who will minister to and rule with Him.

> "To Him who loved us and washed us from our sins in His own blood, and has made us kings and priests to His God and Father, to Him be glory and dominion forever and ever. Amen."
>
> – Revelation 1:5, 6 (NKJV)

> *"And have made us kings and priests to our God; and we shall reign on the earth."*
>
> — Revelation 5:10 (NKJV)

This is an eternal calling, both to be lived out in this age as well as the one to come. As I stated earlier, when God calls us into something, it carries eternal significance. What matters to Him today, will matter to Him tomorrow. We are to live from the eternal reality as kings and priests. It's what we will do forever, so let's get a head start!

DAVIDS DECLARATION

One of the defining moments in David's life was the day that he brought the ark of the covenant back into the city of Jerusalem. Upon receiving the kingdom from the hands of Saul and his lineage, one of the first things David did was bring the ark of the covenant (His presence) back onto the scene (1 Chronicles 13, 15). Before he sets up his own throne, he establishes God's. For some time, the golden box had been in the possession of the Philistines - the exact place it wasn't supposed to be. Philistines represented the works of the flesh, and the presence of God is never to be in the possession of the flesh. It's to be in the hands of lovers, not opposers.

As David ushers the procession of the ark, we notice that he is wearing a linen ephod.

> *"And David was dancing before the Lord with all his might, and David was <u>wearing a linen ephod</u>."*
>
> — 2 Samuel 6:14

The linen ephod was a special article of clothing that was reserved for the priests only.

> "These are the garments which they shall make:
> a breastpiece and an ephod... they shall make
> holy garments for Aaron your brother and his sons,
> thathe may minister as priest to Me."
>
> — Exodus 28:4

During this procession, the priests and people are sacrificing, singing, and playing music. As they worshipped, David, the new king of Israel, was out front dancing before the Lord (2 Samuel 6:14). More than that, he was prophesying. Dancing before the Lord in a "priest only" ephod, he was operating as both a king and a priest. He wore more than a crown, he gladly sported the priestly garment. Brought forth from the fields of Bethlehem to be king, David broke the mold and was prophetically declaring the identity of every believer under the New Covenant. Heaven was making a statement through this young man's act.

I believe this is why David could easily pen the 110th chapter of Psalms, prophesying about Christ coming in the order of Melchizedek. The man after God's own heart (Acts 13) had a revelation of the coming Messiah.

> "The Lord has sworn and will not change His mind, You are
> a priest forever according to the order of Melchizedek"
>
> — Psalm 110:4

The Hebrew word for "order" is dibrah, meaning "manner or mode." Another word we could use is "pattern." Jesus would come after the "manner and pattern" of Melchizedek, who was the priest and king of Salem. He was a royal priest. His very name means "king of righteousness." One of the interesting things about Melchizedek is, before the law was even established through the ministry of Moses, he comes on the scene. Yes, before Moses even establishes the priesthood order (found in Exodus and Leviticus), this priest-king of Salem walks into history (Genesis 14:18-20). So, before there was even a word from God's lips about establishing an order of priesthood, there was one who bore the image of a priest-king. This leads me to believe that the king of Salem (a city that was later named Jerusalem), was none other than the Son of God - it was Jesus. (Many times throughout the Old Testament, the Son of Man appeared to man. We call it Christophany). I believe He was stepping into history to make an early debut of His work and life on the earth as priest-king.

Much of David's life and reign was a glimpse into the New Covenant. Just think about it. During the 33 years of his reign, he sets up the tabernacle (tent) with singers and musicians around it to host day and night worship and prayer. During this time, the sacrifices offered were ones of thanksgiving and praise (Psalm 116:17). Instead of just laying animals on the altar to atone for their sins, David sets up an altar of worship and adoration, where the incense of worship and prayer ascends to God's throne during these 3 decades. A yielded heart would be the primary worship that ascended from the city of David. Sounds like what Paul said in Romans 12:1, "Therefore, I urge you, brothers and sisters, in view of God's mercy, to offer your bodies as a living sacrifice, holy and pleasing to God—this is your true and proper worship." True worship is when we become the sacrifice.

David's act (of prayer, praise, and proclamation) was a prophetic snapshot of what the Lord would do through His Son, the Son of David. No longer would God's people need to trust in the sacrifice of animals and the blood offering, but put their faith in the ultimate sacrifice of the Lamb of God. As His children put their trust in His work, they would be restored as a kingdom of priests, who minister to God in their prayers, praise, and in their proclamation - "you are a chosen race, a royal priesthood, a holy nation, a people for God's own possession, so that you may proclaim the excellencies of Him who has called you out of darkness into His marvelous light" (1 Peter 2:9). I personally believe that what David did during his reign and in his tabernacle, provided a window of grace for Jesus (Son of David) to come and minister on the earth for the same amount of years. The Kingdom that we now receive is expressed by prayer, worship, and an awe-struck heart.

> *"Therefore, since we receive a kingdom which cannot be shaken, let us show gratitude, by which we may offer to God an acceptable service with reverence and awe; for our God is a consuming fire."*
>
> *— Hebrews 12:28, 29 (NASB)*

Because of David's outlandish declaration of joy in dance, his own wife Michal despises him (2 Samuel 6:16). I believe that one of the reasons was due to the fact that she couldn't wrap her "religious" mind around the fact that her husband was wearing a priestly garment, while at the same time holding the office of a king. I can imagine her looking from her "lofty" window with disgust saying, "What in the world is my husband doing? The very thing that he has fought so hard to obtain, he's now going to act like a fool! And to top it off, he's defiling the priesthood by wearing one of their articles of clothing! How could he!?! Does he now think he's a priest?!?"

> *Friends, don't despise someone else's pursuit. Remember Michal, how she despised David's expression of praise - it caused her barrenness. When we choose to despise another's expression of praise to the Lord, we give way to the closing of the womb - the closing of revelation and life in God.*

You see, I don't think Michal despised David simply because of his dance, but mostly because of his declaration. David was an extravagant worshiper and she had seen him in his "high praise." David's dance and outlandish worship was nothing new to her. His radical worship expression wasn't the real issue here. It was simply that she just couldn't wrap her old mindset and religious concepts around the fact that a king was wearing a priestly garment. It was a new day and she just couldn't receive it, and because of it, she suffered barrenness. Because of her unwillingness to cooperate with the new day, the Lord shut her womb (2 Samuel 6:23). At this point, she was showing her true colors as being a daughter of Saul. She was manifesting the religious spirit and couldn't rejoice with the fact that David was ushering in a new day.

As I read this account, I can't help but ask. Is your prayer life provoking the religious spirit and the devils of hell? Is your life in God creating ripple effects in the the spirit?

PRIESTLY FUNCTION

One of the primary functions of the priesthood was to minister to the Lord (Exodus 28:4), in prayer, praise and intercession. In a time of great urgency, Joel calls forth the priest saying "Let the priests, who minister before the Lord…" (Joel 2:17). Exodus 19:8 says the priests are to "come near to the Lord." The posture of the priesthood was a worshipping and praying one. Remember, prayer and praise actually go together and function on the same plane. From this "vertical expression," the priests would stand on behalf of the people, representing the entire nation of Israel. They were to minister to the King in worship and prayer while they administered the Kingdom by intercession. This is why they were called a "kingdom of priests." This priesthood act would be an open display of the goodness and mercy of God to the people.

> *"Through Jesus, therefore, let us continually offer to God a sacrifice of praise—the fruit of lips that openly profess his name. And do not forget to do good and to share with others, for with such sacrifices God is pleased."*
>
> — Hebrews 13:15-16

INTERCESSION

Intercession can be defined, "to act between parties, with a view to reconciling differences." It bears the thought "to stand in the gap."

When two parties are separated, intercession has its open door to operate. And prayer is what facilitates this divine calling of priests. As friends and ambassadors of Christ in the earth, we release the will and purposes of God by our prayers and intercessions. In essence, it's in the place of prayer that we encounter His heart and release His hand. As we have conversation with God, He fills us with His divine will and purposes. He does this to create a cry in us.

> *"The ministry of intercession is about us being filled with the knowledge of what is burning on His heart and, out of the overflow of that knowledge, speaking back to Him what He wants done, knowing that He hears and that He is releasing His power as we ask."*
>
> – *Foundations of Intercession* by Corey Russell

In his letter to the church at Corinth, the apostle Paul tells them that they had received the ministry of reconciliation and then ties it in with the mandate of being an ambassador. These ministries were mandates of high honor. An ambassador's primary mandate is to speak on behalf of another kingdom (nation or people). Just as every nation has an ambassador who represents it, so does the Kingdom of God. Under the authority given by that Kingdom, we represent the value system and the culture as they disperse it to other countries and kingdoms. We are sent to say what the King wants said and to do what the King wants done.

> *"Therefore, we are ambassadors for Christ, as though God were making an appeal through us; we beg you on behalf of Christ, be reconciled to God."*

– 2 Corinthians 5:20 (NASB)

One day as I was sitting at my piano working on some songs, all of a sudden the spirit of intercession came over me and I began to feel a deep burden for a family member. At the time, they were living with us and was in the room next to me. I didn't know what was going on in the natural but in the spirit, I knew there was some major warring going on over their life. I could literally feel the weight of the struggle. Immediately, I had a vision of them asleep in the bed with me standing over top of them, interceding and breaking strongholds off of their life. It was clear that what I was sensing in the spirit was connected to this vision. The Lord had entrusted me with this current battle. This (experience of intercession) lasted for 10-15 minutes. That same day we were standing in the kitchen talking, when they mentioned a dream they had about me praying over top of them. They explained in detail what I had seen in my vision in the next room over. It was so real and almost tangible. I knew right away that this was a divine moment. I never told them I had experienced the same thing, but knew that the Lord had done something amazing. That day, my understanding of intercession changed tremendously. I saw the ministry of intercession as the posture of believers over those who are asleep and at war.

The "sleepers" may be saints in the pews or sinners in the streets. They could very well be pastors behind pulpits or prostitutes in the cities. Whatever the case, there is a generation in need of deliverance from the spirit of the age, of oppression and the torment of the enemy. And we as the body of Christ (His ambassadors in the earth) must arise and take our place in intercession. It's time we begin to adopt and experience the burden of the Lord for a generation, and enter

> *Whether you're a lawyer or a layman, an educator or elder, the ministry of intercession is one of our primary callings in Christ.*

into partnership to see the yoke destroyed. We belong to another Kingdom and we no longer have to tolerate the bullying of the adversary. Our Daddy is stronger! Whether you're a lawyer or a layman, an educator or elder, the ministry of intercession is one of our primary callings in Christ. The Spirit of the Lord is upon Him (Isaiah 61) and as believers in Christ, we have received the same anointing. Arise ambassadors!

WHAT A PRIEST PRAYS LIKE

Intercession is simply saying back to God what He tells us to say. It's about being filled with the thoughts of heaven and bringing those into the present reality. Therefore, at the heart is conversation and dialogue. His voice, His heart, and will is heard and released in our prayers and intercession. In 2 Corinthians 5:20, Paul says we are ambassadors "as though God were making an appeal through us." Appeal in Hebrew is parakaleo, meaning "to call

> *Prayer is about enjoying our identity as priests, standing before and ministering to Him as He ministers to us.*

to one's side, call for, summon, speak to." The Lord is wanting to summon a generation through us. In His goodness, He's sounding His call of mercy and redemption through our lives.

Whether we encounter His heart for the poor in Africa, for the preacher on TV, or the widow down the road, we are to turn those encounters into prayer and intercession. An ambassador will always go to work for the heart of the kingdom he represents. This is a Kingdom principle, that anything given us should be given back to the Lord. For example, when my heart breaks for the unreached people group of Africa, that is an indicator that I need to declare the word of God over them. It may be an injustice like abortion or human trafficking, or it may be the orphans and the widows who capture our heart. Whatever the burden, as we encounter the Lord, we are to believe for others to encounter the same. Sometimes our sowing of tears (in intercession and prayer) will reap for them joy on the other side (Psalm 126:5). Isn't that what Christ did for us. When we couldn't even make our way to the cross, He nailed us there with Him and now gives us the invitation to embrace the crucified lifestyle. His burden became ours.

Many times we can mistake these encounters (with God's heart) as heavy and worrisome burdens that soon weigh us down, but the Lord desires for us to take those burdens and turn them into missiles of intercession. Jesus said "My yoke is easy and my burden is light" (Matthew 11:30). He will often release His (light) burden over us that we can go to bat for the souls of men (1 Timothy 2:1, 2), for intercession was designed to flow like a river. He speaks things to us and we say them back to Him, and so the flow goes. Intercession is powerful, for when those who are oppressed can't find the words to pray, there is a believer down the road or in another country who can bear the burden. This explains why Paul urged the church of Galatia in this manner:

> *"Carry each other's burdens, and in this way you will fulfill the law of Christ."*
>
> — Galatians 6:2 (NIV)

Wow, we can actually fulfill the law of Christ? What was one of the clear ways that Christ fulfilled the law? It was by becoming the mandatory sacrifice that He would reconcile the world unto Himself. Jesus became our great High Priest and took up our case. He bridged the great breach.

As we discussed earlier, to intercede is to go between and stand on behalf of two parties. Jesus made intercession for us meaning that He not only brought us to the Father, but He also brought the Father to us. He brought reconciliation right to our front door. As our great High Priest, He stood in the gap and made us one with the Father. He alone returned us to our favorable positions, seated with Him in heavenly places, as we now partner with Him.

PARTNERING WITH THE LORD

Partnership is at at the heart of intercession. Since the beginning of time, He's had many longings in His heart, and we being one with Him is paramount.

> *"He predestined us for adoption to sonship through Jesus Christ, in accordance with his pleasure and will…"*
>
> *– Ephesians 1:5 (NASB)*

Paul writes to the church at Ephesus about the realm of sonship to emphasize the Lord's heart for partnership. You see, Paul was addressing a Greek crowd in Ephesus that understood adoption. When he used the word "adoption," I'm sure their ears perked up! They understood the power of adoption and being a son in a family. Even in Jewish culture, being a son entitled you to everything the father had. What the father possessed, the son possessed. Upon adoption, every past offense was erased and satisfied through this transaction. It was a legal and final transaction. The adoptee's name changed, his life was restored, and his identity became entirely new. He was a completely new individual! He soon became a sharer and partaker of the nature and possessions of the family he was adopted into. Their resources soon became his. As such, he became a partner in extending and representing the values of that family. Sounds a lot like us huh?

This is the point that Paul is wanting to make to the Ephesus church, that they had been redeemed to the place of divine partnership with God. Being created in His image, He chose, many many years ago, to bring us unto Himself as sons. The position of sonship gives us a glimpse into the reality of partnering with God. What belongs to Him now belongs to me. His resources are mine. When addressing sonship and the issue of (father-son) discipline, the writer of Hebrews gives us the reasoning behind such discipline.

> *"He disciplines us for our good,*
> *so that we may SHARE His holiness."*
>
> *— Hebrews 12:10b (NASB)*

He shares His holiness with us so that we can give out of what we have within. We give out of a redeemed well. 2 Peter 1 says that we are "partakers of His divine nature." We receive that promise and in turn, we bring it to those who are lacking hope, that they may step into their own journey. It's actually then that we work from promise, not merely for it.

> *It's always better to pray as a partaker.*

Intercession is a reality connected to the promises of God. The word from His mouth is connected to the words coming out of ours. E.M. Bounds once said, "Prayer unites with the purposes of God and lays itself out to secure those purposes." When Daniel prayed the famous intercessory prayer in Daniel 9, he was crying out for his people according to the (inspired) promises given to Jeremiah. This young man from Judah was praying the word of God.

> *"…in the first year of his reign, I, Daniel, observed in the books the number of the years which was revealed as the word of the Lord to Jeremiah the prophet for the completion of the desolations of Jerusalem, namely, seventy years. So I gave my attention to the Lord God to seek Him by prayer and supplications, with fasting, sackcloth and ashes. I prayed to the Lord my God and confessed and said, "Alas, O Lord, the great and awesome God, who keeps His covenant and lovingkindness for those who love Him and keep His commandments, we have sinned, committed iniquity, acted wickedly and rebelled, even turning aside from Your commandments and ordinances. Moreover, we have not listened to Your servants the prophets, who spoke in Your name to our kings, our princes, our fathers and all the people of the land."*
>
> *— Daniel 9:2-7*

Daniel's prayer of intercession (standing on behalf of his people) had an eternal value connected to it. The word that had been released from God's mouth added weight to the severity of the hour and brought a heightened awareness of impending judgment if someone didn't turn to the Lord. Daniel was echoing and resounding what had once been released from God's mouth. Nevertheless, Daniel called on the goodness and compassion of God. In one of the most crucial junctures of history, the young man from Judah began to charge the desolation of God's people to the overwhelming character of Yahweh. He met the impending judgments with the compassionate heart of the Creator of the universe, declaring His word. When we pray the promises of God over a people, nation, etc., this is where the prayer of faith is enlisted.

HISTORY AND THE INTERCESSOR

"History belongs to the intercessor"

– Lou Engle

In the words of E.M. Bounds, "Israel as a nation would have met their just destruction and their just fate after their apostasy with the golden calf had it not been for interposition and unfainting importunity of Moses' forty days and forth nights' praying!" ("Complete Works of E.M. Bounds" by E.M. Bounds)

Throughout history, God has partnered with man in releasing His blessing or judgment in the earth. From day one in the garden, it's just the way He set it up. One of the themes of scripture is exactly that - God working with man. The apostle Peter says, "For by these He has granted to us His precious and magnificent promises, so that by them you may become partakers of His divine nature…" (2 Peter 1:4). The Greek word for partakers is koinōnos, meaning "partners, companion, sharer." Partnership (man partaking of His purposes) implies that we cannot do this thing without God and God won't do this thing without us. It's just the wisdom of God

Partnership in prayer was God's idea

to use weak, frail people to accomplish His plans and purposes. In the natural, it always reflects on the coach's wisdom and ability when he can take a weak team of uncoordinated and distracted players and make an excellent group of winners. Same goes for the Lord, for when He takes a group of sincere but broken people and makes us winners, His wisdom and ability shines through. Just as the coach is praised for his ability to lead the group to victory, so the Lord gets the praise and applause of a generation when His team reigns victorious. We see the Lord's coaching ability in the story of Ezekiel.

Standing over a valley of dry and dead bones, the Lord asks Ezekiel, "son of man, can these bones live?" (Ezekiel 37:3). The great God "Jehovah-inquirer" looks to Ezekiel with a "heavy-hitter" question and I'm sure this young prophet is thinking, "Why is He asking me?" Ezekiel quickly turns to the Lord and acknowledges that He surely knows. Yet, the Lord doesn't stop to answer, but instructs Ezekiel to jump in and prophesy to the bones. Yahweh wants human involvement. The Lord makes it clear that He wants man's participation in this soon-coming revival of dry bones. Standing in the midst of death and decay, God knew the destiny, yet He wanted Ezekiel to get it and prophesy. The prophetic gift that He alone had planted in Ezekiel, He wanted to pull it out. I love verse 7, for Ezekiel says, "So I prophesied as I was commanded..." He was commanded to prophesy! God could have easily resolved the "dry bone" issue in a moment with His own word, yet He wanted this young man to speak what was on his heart. So He tells Ezekiel what to say. The Lord plants in Ezekiel what He wants to come out. This is at the heart of intercession - saying to God (and the intended target) what God tells us to say. In essence, Ezekiel was only speaking what He heard. In between God and the valley of bones stood a weak and frail man, yet the Creator of the universe desired his involvement. To God, this young "priest-turned-prophet" had something to bring to the table, and it was his words. He wanted Ezekiel to voice his heart. Friends, this is intercession.

In Genesis 18, we have another glimpse of intercession, as Abraham dialogues with God about the fate of Sodom. Verse 22 says, "but Abraham was still standing before the Lord." The Hebrew word for standing is amad, meaning "to present oneself, to remain." So, while the angels went about the Lord's business, Abraham presented himself before the Lord. It's the same word used when the priests would stand before the Lord to minister and make intercession, as well as when the priests would present the offering for sin (atonement). There is a prophetic message here. Abraham (the father of nations who was credited as a "righteous" man) presented himself before the Lord (as a priest and/or offering) to satisfy the Lord. However, he doesn't do it by throwing himself on an altar, but reminding the Lord of the power of righteousness.

Soon God comes down in reply to the cries going up. We see that Abraham begins to lift his voice to the Lord, asking that He would spare the city for 50 righteous people. The Lord agrees but can't find that many. Father Abraham then asks, "What about 45 righteous?" Still, that many can't be found. As the countdown to "find the righteous" continues, the Lord finally agrees to withhold His wrath for 10 righteous (18:32). This reveals the truth that the power of intercession isn't just in the numbers, it's in the righteousness. In the life of Christ, the weight of one righteous person overwhelms the weight of sin and iniquity.

God wouldn't destroy the city until Lot and his family were completely gone from the scene (Genesis 19:22). Lot's name in the Hebrew means "covering." Lot provided a covering for the land and the Lord wouldn't release His wrath on the city until His friends had escaped to the village of Zoar. I believe this adds weight to the reason why Jesus called us the "salt of the earth" (Matthew 5:13-15). Salt is known for preserving things and drawing the flavor out of food. Perhaps Jesus is saying over His church, "You are called to preserve cities and pull out the flavor of your sphere of influence." Covered in the righteousness of God, we are to stand and call our friends, family, and cities into their eternal destiny by the ministry of intercession. We can all attest to the fact that angels stood ready to release the judgments of God on our behalf, but there was a perfect Man who interceded for our broken lives. The incense of His life ascended before God as a pleasing aroma. He is the perfect example. He is the Great High Priest!

MINISTRY OF RECONCILIATION

Through intercession and by reminding the Lord of His promises, we preserve the will of God in the earth. Intercession is connected to promise. Oh, the importance of knowing the Word. This is why the apostle Peter says, "He has granted to us His precious and magnificent promises, so that by them you may become partakers (partners in intercession)…" (2 Peter 1:4). We are given promises in order to partake (partner) with God to see them come into fruition. In his letter to the Corinth church, Paul calls intercession the "ministry of reconciliation." It's the divine ministry of bringing two parties together. What once was breached and broken, we can partner with God and begin to call people and places into their eternal destiny.

> *"Now all these things are from God, who reconciled us to Himself through Christ and gave us the ministry of reconciliation, namely, that God was in Christ reconciling the world to Himself, not counting their trespasses against them, and He has committed to us the word of reconciliation."*
>
> — 2 Corinthians 5:18, 19 (NASB)

Although a mystery, every believer has received this ministry of reconciliation. Intercession isn't some elect ministry for the "elite," it's for everyday ordinary people. The priesthood isn't just a call for the guy who pastors a church or oversees a congregation. Friends, the priesthood is a call for everyone who believes in the work of the Great High Priest, Jesus. Every stay at home mom, working dad, businessman, athlete, musician, whether you've been saved decades or just days, God sees you as a priest. His calling for you is to stand in the gap, to intercede and stand on behalf of others. In essence, we've been called to talk to God. Intercession is what got you in the Kingdom and it's the very ministry that He is urging us to take up. Take your place on the wall as a king and a priest and declare the word of the Lord over your home, your city, and the area He has entrusted to you!

In Isaiah 62, He tells His watchmen (intercessors) to remind Him of His promises. When the God of the universe speaks, He's just looking for someone to grab ahold and release those promises back into the atmosphere. He's the God whose word does not return void (Isaiah 55:11), and it's path is right back to the throne as we release it to Him. It's just the way He set it up. When we stand as priests and kings before the Great King, we can remind Him of the value and destiny of our cities, our schools, the nations, etc. This is why it's important to know the destiny of our cities, so we can call it back to God. He already knows it, but just like Ezekiel, He wants us to say it back to Him. That's the mystery of intercession. I believe the main reason why Abraham and Lot were crying out for Sodom and Gomorrah, was because they understood that the city had eternal promise and purpose attached to it. Lot had personally seen the similarities of the garden of Eden in it (Genesis 13:10). I'm sure he was warring inside as he knew the destiny was contrary to what the Lord had shown him. Friends, he has placed destiny inside of each of these spheres, and He wants us to hear, see, and say them back to Him. This is divine partnership. Isaiah had a revelation of Jerusalem's eternal destiny as a great city - a city of praise. Out of this promise, Isaiah urges the watchmen (intercessors) to call it back into it's original purpose.

> *"On your walls, O Jerusalem, I have appointed watchmen; all day and all night they will never keep silent. You who remind the Lord, take no rest for yourselves; and give Him no rest until He establishes and makes Jerusalem a praise in the earth."*
>
> — Isaiah 62:6, 7 (NASB)

When both of my children (Luke and Olivia) were born, I asked the Lord to give me insight into their destiny and calling. I remember praying over my son Luke on the way home from the hospital saying, "Lord show me what You're calling Luke into." I wanted to be passionate about stewarding their lives in prayer. I personally like being specific in prayer and I imagined, what better way to pray for my kids than to call them into their eternal destiny and calling - to agree with what God says over them. Although I am still learning about their specific callings, I have a very specific prayer I declare over each of them. As I've stated throughout this book, I call this "praying from identity." In fact, when I pray by understanding someone's destiny, I take a position of thanking the Lord rather than merely asking the Lord. For example, I will say, "Lord, I thank You that You have called Olivia to minister to You through song. I thank You that You have filled her mouth with a new song and that through her life, many would see, fear, and put their trust in You." When I receive the revelation of one's calling in life, I pray from His view of maturity, rather than my limited sight of immaturity.

Every time we speak what we hear (in intercession) we are stirring up our faith. We not only remind Him but we also remind ourselves. Paul said that "faith comes by hearing and hearing by the word of Christ" (Romans 10:17). It's about hearing His word and speaking it out. The sound of His voice is released through ours and we are strengthened. A lifestyle of this (by doing it over and over) fortifies our inner man and builds walls of resolve in serving Jesus. Subtle and small installments of declaring the word will prove its power.

The Lord is calling His body into the realm of ascended prayer. He is urging us to see our prayers and intercession as descending bombs on an intended target. When the United States military chooses to fire a missile into an area, they have an intended target. In their inherit authority given by the United States, they know exactly where they are going. The authority is there, the confidence is there, and most

> *Every time we choose to speak what we hear (in intercession) we are stirring up our faith.*

importantly - the order from a higher authority is there. It's the same idea when we partner with God in prayer and intercession. We get His heart, we hear His voice, and we launch the heavenly missiles into our intended target! This is what happens when we partner with God in intercession. We begin to launch faith-filled missiles into enemy-saturated ground. We live in the greatest Kingdom with the most powerful weapons and resources. May we activate what has been given us.

AUTHORITY IN PRAYER

"The heavens are the heavens of the Lord, but the earth He has given to the sons of men."

— Psalm 115:16 (NASB)

When God created the world, He gave authority to mankind. He put man in charge over the works of His hands - "Then God said, Let Us make man in Our image, according to Our likeness; and let them rule over the fish of the sea and over the birds of the sky and over the cattle and over all the earth, and over every creeping thing that creeps on the earth" (Genesis 1:26). Two verses later He calls man to "Be fruitful and increase in number; fill the earth and subdue it (1:28). In other translations, another word for rule is "to have dominion." He built the house and handed the keys over to man. From day one, He gave man a kingly identity, a royal job description. He didn't just say "sit back and watch Me rule." He gave us the mandate to do so. This is part of the mystery of the gospel, that God (infinite and perfect in nature) would choose weak and broken people like you and me to take care of what He designed. He is a God who trusts people. Amazing!

So, when Adam and Eve sinned, they handed over the keys to the house. The eternal authority they had been given was forfeited in a single moment. The grave sin of Adam and Eve was not that they simply disobeyed God, but they actually changed masters. In their obedience to the serpent, the earth came under submission of a new leader. From that moment forward (before the cross), Satan had full reign over the earth. He became its ruler. In an attempt to retain his authority, Satan tempted Christ with things like, "I will give You all this domain and its glory; for it has been handed over to me, and I give it to whomever I wish. Therefore if You worship before me, it shall all be Yours" (Luke 4:6 NASB). He could tempt Christ with the earth's domain and glory because it actually belonged to Him. In addition, Christ could be tempted because He was flesh. And this is the beauty of the gospel, that the Creator wrapped Himself in flesh to give His life into the hands of men and women, even into the realm of Satan's temptation. God required a man to redeem mankind and Jesus stepped up to the plate! He didn't stand back from the clinches of mankind, rather He threw Himself right in the middle of it. It was His divine choice...

> *"No one has taken it away from Me, but I lay it down on My own initiative. I have authority to lay it down, and I have authority to take it up again. This commandment I received from My Father."*
>
> — John 10:18 (NASB)

Because God gave authority of the earth over to mankind, it would take a human to get it back. The Greek word for "domain" in Luke 4:6 is exousia, meaning "power of choice, regal authority, crown." The Godhead made the glorious choice to yield the Son's life as the perfect ransom for restoration of authority to mankind. They wanted to restore kingly authority back into the hands of men.

> *"Therefore, since the children share in flesh and blood, He Himself likewise also partook of the same, that through death He might render powerless him who had the power of death, that is, the devil, and might free those who through fear of death were subject to slavery all their lives."*
>
> – Hebrews 2:14, 15 (NASB)

So, when Christ entered the domain of Satan full of the Holy Spirit, armed with forty days of fasting and carrying a word (of affirmation) from His Father, the authority would soon change hands. In Satan's attempt to remain supreme as the ruler of the earth, he goes head to head with the Son of Man (Luke 4:2). What decisions are made in these forty days will tell the fate of the earth, for eternity. I'm sure the angels and heavens hosts are leaning over the balcony, as they watch the 40 day showdown. The Father is fully confident in His Son, that He will choose the way laid before Him. For it was the "voice of confidence" that launched Him there (Matthew 3:17).

As you know, Satan lobs 3 temptations at Him, all dealing with food, life, and worship (oh, how these are the same temptations we encounter today). Jesus answers the temptations with the sure will of God. The Word made flesh answers with the word. In essence, Jesus is trumping the father of lies with the powerful truth of His

Father. Christ goes on to pass the wilderness test, only to be nailed to the cross and to fully redeem mankind to the rightful place of authority in the earth. Jesus, in His humanity, wrestled Satan to the ground and took the keys of dominion from him. Moments after His resurrection, He boldly declares, "All authority has been given to Me in heaven and on earth." That's right, <u>all authority in heaven and on earth</u>. All authority means that Satan has none! Zero… Zilch! Jesus didn't just take the celestial (heavenly) realm, but the earth as well. He took the "whole key ring" of dominion from the devil. He ripped it from his cold, dead hands.

He then charges His disciples to "Go therefore and make disciples of all the nations, baptizing them in the name of the Father and the Son and the Holy Spirit, teaching them to observe all that I commanded you…" (28:19, 20). In essence, He is saying, "Listen guys, I just wrestled Satan to the ground, took back the keys of earthly dominion, and now I am giving them back to you. Now, under my leadership, go disciple and take back dominion for yourself. Make disciples, teach them, baptize them." In His charge, Jesus is taking them back to the garden saying, "Be fruitful and multiply." His call is to restore the garden of Eden of knowing God and releasing God in the earth. In essence, He is saying "take what I have placed in you and done for you, and GO! GO, take dominion that belongs to you!" I must show you this verse again…

> "The heavens are the heavens of the Lord, but the earth He has given to the sons of men."
>
> — Psalm 115:16 (NASB)

Discipleship is what enacts and sustains the authority of God in a person, region, city, etc. It's what brings His authority on the scene as an active lifestyle, establishing and causing His Kingdom and will to be done on earth as it is in heaven. As the church realizes the authority that we have to enact and establish things in the Spirit, our prayer lives will soar.

In his book *Spirit Wars*, Kris Vallotton writes:

> *"Jesus told Christians to disciple nations. The way that principalities gain authority over a nation is for believers to vacate their God-given spheres (regions)."*

Many times we look at the word "GO" and immediately think that we must jump on a plane and do a mission trip. Many equate the going to literally putting our feet to the ground and marching down to the nearest street corner. Although there is much truth to that, it's not the full truth of what Jesus is saying. "GO" in the Greek means "to transfer, carry over, continue in one's journey." It speaks of receiving and releasing the truth of what He was saying. He wanted the truth of gaining "all authority" from the devil to "be carried over and transferred" into the disciples' life and journey, and He wants it to do the same in ours. What Jesus obtained, He wants to instill into mankind. He has received it from the Father and now wants to give it away to us as a free gift of grace and salvation.

Whether we stand and pray, or sit before Him and intercede for the nations, we are taking that "all authority" and releasing it in the form of words. By the work of the great High Priest, we have been given legal jurisdiction to enact the Kingdom of God in earth. When Paul used words like "justification" and being "made right," he was using legal terms. This is a legal right we have. In his letter to the Corinth church, Paul says we have the "ministry of reconciliation" (2 Cor. 5:18). We have received reconciliation, and now stand with a glorious responsibility to use it. Therefore, He asks that we stand and join in with Him.

He wants this victory mindset to get involved in our prayer life. He wants us to think like kings and priests and pray from that place. This is part of the ascended lifestyle.

He eagerly desires all nations for His inheritance (Psalm 2), and invites us to join in on the prayer meeting (Matthew 9:38). We join with Him by asking in prayer, and thanking Him by intercession. He doesn't just beseech the Father for the nations by Himself, He asks us to join in with Him, asking that He would send "GO'ers" for the gospel . What a joyful thing. This releases joy in our intercession!

In Christ, He has given us the ministry of intercession as a primary means to release and mediate His resources (mercy, justice, power, wisdom). This is a ministry that we have inherited now (in this age) and forever (in the age to come). No better time to invest in the eternal than now… Let's stand with Him!

six
Bold Before the Throne

*"Let us therefore come **boldly unto the throne of grace**, that we may obtain mercy, and find grace to help in time of need."*

— Hebrews 4:16

It was a hot summer day at my parents' house, and we were playing some paintball. With my dad and all of the Atwood boys, it was a day of merciless and intense hunting, and maybe even more intense hiding. If you've ever played a good game of paintball, you know what I'm talking about. It's the ultimate mix of survival, hunting, and just plain fear of getting pegged by that little colored ball. As the battles drew to an end, we all headed back to the house to enjoy some "bro time." As I walked in, I headed straight to the refrigerator to grab a cold drink. Without any hesitation, I flung open the door and grabbed the first thing in my sight - a giant, glorious gallon of sweet tea. (If anyone knows my mother, she makes the largest and sweetest iced tea this side of the Mississippi.) I didn't ask for permission to open the refrigerator to enjoy a drink of the tea. No, friends, I just barged into their kitchen with no apologies, ripped open that cold fridge door, and grabbed whatever I desired. To be honest, I can't remember the last time that I actually asked permission to do such a thing in my parents' house. I believe most of us can connect with this.

WHAT IS TRUE IN THE NATURAL, IS TRUE IN THE SPIRITUAL

Never have I gone to my dad's house and asked if I could enter. Nor have I ever trembled, hoping that he would allow me to cross his threshold. I haven't experienced any of this simply because I know that I am invited into his abode. Whether it's a sunny day, or a late and rainy night, I am always welcome. No matter if I'm in a season of success or one of struggle, his door is always open to me. With this, I always come on in and pull up a chair. And yes, many times I grab a glass of sweet tea. The cupboards are wide open for me to take what I need and his living area is free for me to lounge and just hang out. His arms are always open to me any time of any day. It's always been like that. Why? Because I am his son. I am old man Atwood's boy, therefore I am free to enter. Any other response (than wide open invitation and acceptance from Him) would seem absurd to me.

This is how Abba Father, our (heavenly) Daddy wants us (His children) to see Him. We are welcome into His living room and He has opened up His abode to us. He's placed it on the inside of us. He wants to break off false and fragmented images, and exchange them for the glorious reality that we have a "Father in heaven" who delights in us. He's a Father who sits above the circle of the earth and in the midst of His children. Since all effective prayer begins with right perspective, He wants to trade us out of our outdated perspectives and bring us into a heavenly one. We ask according to how we see. Therefore, He wants to smash the lies and the filter of fear that has led us to inward captivity, and bring us into the truth that we are loved and accepted. The Holy Spirit wants to gives us ears to hear what Paul declared in Romans 8:

> *He wants to break off the false and fragmented images we have of Him, and exchange them for the glorious reality that we have a "Father in heaven."*

> *"For you have not received a spirit of slavery leading to fear again, but you have received a spirit of adoption as sons by which we cry out, "Abba! Father!" The Spirit Himself testifies with our spirit that we are children of God, and if children, heirs also, heirs of God and fellow heirs with Christ, if indeed we suffer with Him so that we may also be glorified with Him."*
>
> — Romans 8:15

In Luke 15, Jesus tells us that the Father "sees, feels compassion for him, runs, embraces, and kisses" His sons. These five affections of the father give us insight into how God saw us and continues to see us in our frailty and weakness. Nowhere in the affections of the Father is there a coat of condemnation that He puts on us to bear. Rather, He is clothing us with royalty. His yoke is easy and His burden is light. Sometimes I think this reality has become a "prodigal message." May the children of God run back home to the truth that we are His.

> "So he got up and came to his father. But while he was still a long way off, his father saw him and felt compassion for him, and ran and embraced him and kissed him. And the son said to him, 'Father, I have sinned against heaven and in your sight; I am no longer worthy to be called your son.' But the father said to his slaves, 'Quickly bring out the best robe and put it on him, and put a ring on his hand and sandals on his feet; and bring the fattened calf, kill it, and let us eat and celebrate; for this son of mine was dead and has come to life again; he was lost and has been found.' And they began to celebrate."
>
> — Luke 15:20-24 (NASB)

One day I was reading the prayer that Jesus taught His disciples to pray (Matthew 6:9). He begins the petition by saying "Our Father in heaven, hallowed be Your name…" As I began to pray through it, the Holy Spirit spoke to me and said, "Do you realize that even the angels can't call Him Father, but you can?". I was floored. That had to be one of the most powerful things that He has ever said to me. Think about that. As glorious as the hosts of heaven are, they can't connect their Creator with the powerful truth that He is their Father. Although they perpetually enjoy the power and majesty of God around the throne, they don't have the honor and privilege to utter His intimate and personal heart as "Abba Daddy." This is one truth that we have the glorious privilege of declaring. From a heart of awe-filled gratitude, we are invited to declare and enjoy this infinite Creator as our Abba - He is Daddy! No other created being has that amazing privilege.

Oh, how many times do we view our heavenly Father in a distorted view. How often do we think that we have to tiptoe to the front door and hope, just hope, that He is in a good mood. Or maybe, we think if we have a good day or a great week that He will let us enter. Often times do we think His acceptance rests on our performance. We need to change our mind concerning this!

Although I firmly believe in living consecrated and set apart unto obedience, never do I want to think that it gets me access to the Father. Although my fellowship and encounters benefit from living holy and set apart, my relationship (the value of relating to Him) does not. Jesus and Jesus alone fixed my relationship. I couldn't relate to Him by keeping the written law, and we know what happened there - we failed miserably. You and I were jacked up and beyond "self-help". We needed a Man of utter perfection and unconditional love to come and rescue us from the pit of our sin and rebellion. We needed a Man to come and acquaint Himself with the weakness and frailty of the human frame, to bring us back into alignment with the Father. And praise God, He did! (Isaiah 53:3; Hebrews 4:15). As Bill Johnson once said, "He took what we deserved, so we could get what He deserved."

I have a son who will soon be crossing over into the teenage years. He's such a kind, caring, and amazing young man. He always considers others and looks to bring the best out of everyone. Yet, sometimes he chooses to do things that are out of his character. He may push the envelope of obedience, or maybe even just push his little sister to the edge of insanity. Whatever the case, these moments come up and will more than likely continue to surface. However, in any of the "life happenings" and various behaviors,

Luke never ceases to be my son. Never do I look at him in disgust and say, "That's it, you're out of the family." He will forever be my son and he will forever carry on the Atwood name. This is who he is. Although I may choose to discipline him, he is still an Atwood, and I will always view him as such. He doesn't have to "perform" or work to get my approval. He already has it.

Don't let the accusations of the enemy keep you from going into the prayer closet, but let the affirmations of the Father drive you into it. A delightful Papa is awaiting your entry. Jesus taught us to begin prayer with God as "our heavenly Father" because He wanted the children to have the right perspective up front. He knew it was more important to understand whom we're praying to than what we were praying. As we understand that "Our Father in heaven" wants to hear from us and speak to us, it changes everything.

THE GREAT HIGH PRIESTS' GREAT PRAYER

Jesus makes the Trinitarian desire so clear when He prays one of His last and most famous prayers in John 17. I believe this prayer to be the most vivid and vulnerable prayer recorded in the Scriptures. For an entire chapter, we are given a front seat to the historic and intercessory prayer of the Great High Priest Himself. We are brought into a prayer meeting that changed history. Praying in the garden of Gethsemane, it's the expressed deep desire of the Father, Son, and Holy Spirit. John Piper states that "Jesus' final great prayer in John 17 has been considered the quintessential chapter to study the heart of Jesus. Some church fathers have declared it to be the holiest chapter among the scriptures because in these verses the heart of Jesus is laid bare". He calls it "the greatest prayer in the world," and goes on to say...

> *"What hung in the balance was the glory of God's grace and the salvation of the world. The success of Jesus' mission to earth depended on Jesus's prayer and the answer given. He prayed with reverence and his request was given."*

I couldn't agree more. This prayer alone carries the weight of desire for both the Godhead and humanity. It has its roots in the garden of Eden, where God and man dwelled together, where they were one. Interestingly, we see heaven and earth come together in its 26 verses.

Remember, this chapter can also be named the "priestly prayer," implying that Jesus is making intercession for mankind. And as the perfect Great High Priest who only prays the perfect will of the Father, He's going to get this prayer answered! The Father promised Him the nations as His inheritance (Psalm 2:8), and He will get it. If it means climbing that hill and being nailed to the cross before Him, He is going to have a people wholly His.

As Jesus is praying and declaring His heart's desire, He makes one most important request. This petition that He makes before the Father is at the heart of intimacy. If there was ever a statement that explains the Trinity's desire to draw close and intimately know mankind, this would be the one. In verse 24, Jesus prays, "Father, I desire that they also, whom You have given Me, be with Me where I am, so that they may see My glory which You have given Me, for

You loved Me before the foundation of the world." Father I desire... wow! Jesus has desires that He would find paramount to pray right before His death. Before He would climb the hill and embrace the cross, He would first utter a heartfelt prayer that would get Him possession of His inheritance. The word desire here means "to love, delight in, find pleasure in." This desire is "on fire desire", no less than holy burning love! In essence, He is saying, "Father I find pleasure in them being (close) with Me where I am (in the throne room), that they would see My glorious beauty and splendor." This is not some weak little unspoken request - this is effectual fervent prayer directly from a heart that's on fire. It's the great desire of the Godhead, crying out for the nearness of humanity. He wants His inheritance seated with Him. He prayed it and He will get it!

I would have loved to have been there as "God in flesh" prayed to His Father. From this garden, God the Son is pouring out His heart to God the Father. I can only imagine the intensity and longing of His voice as He poured out His heart before the One in whom He delighted. Just perhaps the drops of blood that He sweat were formed out of painful desire - a desire that wrenches your heart and your whole being. One that moved Him to march up that hill and enter that grave, only to break its power and bring us into the reality of this prayer, that we may be with Him where He is.

Might I add that this prayer is not just a priestly prayer, but one of a passionate bridegroom. This prayer is drenched with desire and a burning passion to bring us back to the place of first love, where we can love Him as we were created, experiencing Him as our friend and brother, sharing our love with no other. He prayed in the garden to bring us back to the garden (of Eden) reality. This is the defining mark of His great (John 17) prayer.

In looking at this passage, I want to focus on the words "be with Me where I am, so that they may see My glory." Remember, this is an open display of the Son's desired closeness and we are given a glorious glimpse into it. He wants friends and lovers, not distant slaves. He wants nearness. With Him in heavenly places, He wants us to see His glory. He wants to bring us before Him and wow us with the power of His majesty. He doesn't just desire that we be in the vicinity of it, but to be right on top of it.

How many of us go to a fireworks show and park miles away, only to see faint sparks in the distance? Do we stop and watch its glamour from behind the veil of rolling hills? No, of course not, we want to be right on top of it. We want the glare of the colors to light up our eyeballs. We want to see the intricate detail of every flash and color. Beloved, we were made to see and experience His glory. We were designed to be right in the middle of heaven's glorious fireworks show. We were made to see His beauty and glory. John boasts of the sounds of thunder and flashes of lightning that are around the throne (Revelation 4:5). He trumpets the activity of songs and sounds being declared that He is holy, He is worthy. He is the Lamb and He wants us to know it. The Trinity wants us to live from the place of encounter and awestruck wonder. I can hear Him saying something like this, "God, bring them close enough to be overwhelmed with the beauty and majesty of who I am. May they sense and experience the love that You and I share - the glory of God's desire and affection."

PRAYING FROM THE KNOWLEDGE OF GOD

Prayer pulls up a seat to behold the beauty of God. In fact, prayer is a form of beholding. As we take time and talk with the God of jasper and sardius (Revelation 4:3), our hearts are transformed from glory to glory (2 Corinthians 3:18). We become what we behold. Once we get a glimpse of His beauty, we can pray from that place. The Lord commanded the Old Testament priests to dress and adorn with glorious (beautiful) apparel because He wanted them to stand and minister from the identity of glory and beauty (Exodus 28:2). In the same way, He wants our ministry to reflect the beauty of His Son.

As we behold in prayer, we can declare and ask things with conviction that there is a glorious God interacting with us. We must condition ourselves to pray from the knowledge of God. When prayer is laced with the glory of God, it becomes engaging and alive.

He doesn't ask that we tiptoe around the perimeter of His throne room. He never urged us to stay back until we have it all together. Rather, He urges us to run in with reckless abandonment, to "come up here" and behold the beauty of God. He wants to show us His fullness and wow us with the majesty of His power. He isn't at all shameful or bashful, nor is He reserved in His display. He longs more than any human being, to bring us into a vibrant and growing knowledge of Himself. Friends, He placed the most powerful exclamation on His desire when He nailed His perfect Son to a rugged cross on behalf of a broken people - and said, "It is finished" (John 19:30). A large part of the "finishing" is that mankind no longer has to fulfill all the written laws to come before Him, but now we can, (through faith in Jesus) come barging into the courts of the Lord.

In essence, when Jesus rent the veil, He was making the boldest statement any prophet or teacher could ever make. The Son of Man was saying, "It is finished and it is open, Come on in!"

Beloved, it's time that we experience the power of the rent veil in our prayer lives. May we hear it in our heart. May we experience the truth of the Father's open living room. May we go beyond just quoting it from a Sunday school head knowledge. It's time we pray, move, and live with a "torn veil" reality. Jesus was declaring that He wanted mankind to be with Him. He wanted conversation with man and once and for all, He finished the task of making it a reality. Scripture tells us that the earth trembled and shook at this great event of God opening up the throne room (Matthew 27:51). It's time we begin to tremble with the revelation that it's open. Just as He invited Moses into the burning bush, He is urging us to come in to His burning throne room. He is a consuming fire and says, "Come close with boldness."

So, what are you waiting for? It's time we begin to pray from an ascended mindset, knowing that we have full access to the throne of God. Any time of any day, even when we're in any mood or setting, we are invited in. He hears and loves to hearken to our voice. Will you go before the throne in boldness? Will you but enter past the rent veil and enter into the power of that promise?

> *"While Jesus was here on earth, He offered prayers and pleadings, with a loud cry and tears, to the One who could rescue him from death. And God heard His prayers because of His deep reverence for God."*
>
> – Hebrews 5:7 (NLT)

Throughout the Old Testament, the ark of the covenant was the object of God's presence. The ark was a small box overlaid with gold that God commanded Moses to construct. It was in conjunction with the elaborate temple that Yahweh Himself instructed to build (Exodus 37:1-9). As the nation of Israel sought conquest and rest in the land of Canaan, the priests would carry it on their journey (Joshua 3:3, 6).

JESUS - THE ARK OF COVENANT

Jesus was the "very ark of covenant," God in flesh. He was and is God's full presence. Colossians 1:19 tells us that it "pleased God for all of His fullness to dwell inside" of this Man. Quite frankly, God the Father couldn't fit anymore of Himself inside of His Son. Jesus was God maxed out!

Jesus, in His great mercy, presented not only man to God, but also God to man. That is a glorious truth to rejoice in. When we were too broken and frail and dirty to crawl, God Himself took up flesh and came running to us. With redemption in His heart and fire in His eyes, He split the very curtain that would separate the "elite" and the common ordinary man from encountering Him. With the pounding blow of the cross, the Godhead declared, "I want to dwell with man, and I will give My best in order to do so." We see that laying open of the body of Christ would open up the presence of God, making His heart accessible to those who would dare seek it.

The boldness that He beckons us to (when entering His presence) is only a direct reflection of His boldness to redeem us. The Father doesn't just permit us into His throne room, He invites us. With open arms and a vulnerable heart, the Lord has swung wide the secret place for every believer. The most fervent in prayer are often those the most bold in the throne room, for they've experienced the power of the rent veil. It's touched their hearts and they live to touch His.

My prayer is that every child of God would be awakened to the reality of the torn veil. I pray that we would come boldly before our Father and take our place as heirs with God and co-heirs with Christ. I pray that we would like never before, pray from the place of being seated with Christ. I pray we would come boldly before the throne!

seven
Praying in the Spirit

This is probably my favorite subject when it comes to prayer and probably the most valuable in my journey of walking with Jesus. I grew up in the Pentecostal arena, so I've been around it most of my life. However, I never really understood, nor did I have a desire to do it, until my senior year in high school. I had always heard that praying in the Spirit was one of the gifts that would take you to the next level in Your relationship with Christ, and that's exactly what I wanted. I was tired of going through the same mundane motions of boredom and being disengaged from God. For too long, the earthly pleasures had stolen my affection and it was time to get serious about following Jesus. So, in my simple hunger to draw closer to Him, I began to seek this gift (by prayer and reading Scripture about receiving more of the Holy Spirit). I decided I was going to jump in with both feet and knew if I wanted more of Him, He had to have more of me.

It wasn't long before I received this gift of praying in the Spirit. It came on a Sunday evening in a corporate setting in Stanford, KY.

The moment I received my prayer language, everything changed. It was like fire released in my bones and light into my mind. Aside from receiving Jesus, it's the greatest gift given me.

Since this gift has had such a profound impact on my life, for a few years now I've made it my goal to pray in the Spirit for at least one hour a day. I do this in all kinds of settings - in my vehicle while driving, under my breath at the gym working out, in the prayer room, around the house, etc. During this time, I've noticed that my heart's capacity for encounter and understanding has enlarged. The ability to hear and discern the voice of God has greatly increased. Many times, I can feel my heart being tenderized as I do it. Most of the times, it doesn't include "fireworks," just small installments of His nearness. Therefore, there hasn't been one moment that has been wasted. Being intentional this way has paid big dividends.

POWER OF PRAYING IN THE SPIRIT

Praying in tongues is a multi-faceted gift, meaning it carries many powerful benefits. From increased revelation to the building of faith, it's a gift that I'm convinced will take any believer to a new level in God. One of the books that's clearest on the power and importance of being filled with the Spirit is the book of Acts. Chapter 1 gives us the mission of praying in the Spirit, as Acts 2 gives us the manifestation of it. We see the manifest power in the book of Acts when the Holy Spirit visited the praying community in the upper room. As they waited and postured themselves in prayer, the Holy Spirit descended in great power. At Jesus' command to go to Jerusalem (Luke 24), the prayer detonator was being set and in due time, the Holy Spirit fire and explosion would be released. Acts 1:8 tells us:

> *"You will receive power when the Holy Spirit has come upon you; and you shall be My witnesses both in Jerusalem, and in all Judea and Samaria, and even to the remotest part of the earth."*
>
> *– Acts 1:8*

On Pentecost, Jesus promised that the apostles and company would be filled with the overwhelming power, strength, and ability of the Holy Spirit. The resurrected Christ gives them hope of an increased presence of His power. It would be the same power that dwells in Christ. Not a diminished power, but the same power and glory of Christ.

> *"And if the Spirit of him who raised Jesus from the dead is living in you, He who raised Christ from the dead will also give life to your mortal bodies because of His Spirit who lives in you."*
>
> *– Romans 8:11 (NIV)*

One of the Greek definitions of "power" highlights the idea of "power consisting in or resting upon armies, forces, and hosts." Jesus declares that the power that rests upon entire military forces will rest in and upon the believer. To give some context of what the apostles would have heard Jesus saying, eastern armies were highly dominant and controlling over their territory and people. Their force, feared and dreaded by many, was recognized throughout the known world. Their power wasn't one that anyone wanted to challenge.

They were the dominating force of the day. So, Jesus is sending a promise of power that would drive back the opposers. A kind of power that rests on forces of troops. One that would dominate the realms and inevitably drive back the opposer. This is what's living on the inside and should be manifesting on the outside!

The (primary) Greek word for power is dynamis meaning "strength, power, ability, might." It's where we get the word dynamite and points to a supernatural enablement or a divine quickening. The potential of dynamite is amazing. Its most common use is to destroy structures and dismantle (entire) massive landscapes - those that couldn't be moved other than with the use of dynamite. When you study dynamite, you see that it has several interesting elements to it: First of all, it's very small in size yet carries an amazing amount of power - enough to pull a massive structure off of its foundation. Secondly, the substance that carries the fire power has to be harnessed in a container with absorbent (earth-based) material. If not, it is dangerous to have around and doesn't serve its original purpose.

The same power that rests in Christ is instilled into these little containers called bodies and we now carry the ability to move mountains and structures off their foundations. We have a mountain-moving, foundation-shaking type of dynamic power. Paul says we are "destroying speculations and every lofty thing raised up against the knowledge of God, and we are taking every thought captive to the obedience of Christ…" (2 Corinthians 10:5 NASB). When we activate this power-filled gift by praying in the Spirit, we access the dynamite that will bring down thoughts that exalts itself against the knowledge of God. It has the power and ability to pull entire stronghold off of its foundation. Those thoughts that wage war against the nature and goodness of God are brought down as we release our prayer language. There may be fortified cities that can only be destroyed by praying with this type of dynamite power. He wants to couple His dynamite power with our earthly vessel and move structures and strongholds that have been hindering us from receiving breakthrough. All over the earth, He wants to ignite something that is explosive. He wants to do it in our weak and frail "earthen vessels."

> *He wants to couple His dynamite power with our earthly vessel and move structures and strongholds that have been hindering us from receiving breakthrough.*

> *"But we have this treasure in earthen vessels, so that the surpassing greatness of the power(dynamis) will be of God and not from ourselves; we are afflicted in every way, but not crushed; perplexed, but not despairing; persecuted, but not forsaken; struck down, but not destroyed; always carrying about in the body the dying of Jesus, so that the life (zoe, vigorus and on fire life) of Jesus also may be manifested in our body."*
>
> – 2 Corinthians 4:7-10

I imagine every time we pray in tongues we are taking that dynamite power and storing it in our inner man - man's inward depository. There will be mountains that need to be moved and according to how you have filled your inner man depository will determine your breakthrough. And let me ask you, do you need a little or a big breakthrough?

OUR WORDS ARE SEEDS

So then, how do we access such power? If God raised Jesus from the dead to make us alive, how do I come into contact with this dynamite life? I'm so glad you asked! Before I answer that, let me first establish something. The words we speak are seeds. Whenever you release words from your mouth, you are sowing seed into whatever it falls upon. In most cases, the soil it falls upon is people. The words have to go somewhere. Think about that. God's words have eternal value and resonance, and we are made in His image. So, perhaps our words carry the same reality. Just a thought!

So, Jesus taught this principle in Luke 8:11, saying, "The seed is the word of God." This means that every word that God speaks has seed potential and it will reap fruit. The question is, where will His word land and sprout its intended foliage. Do we want our "word-seed" to create life? Do we want to pack power in our words? Then friends, I urge you to pray in the Spirit.

WE NEED POWER

It was on a Sunday morning at 4:30 A.M. that I woke up to a loud beep. (At 4:30 A.M., everything is much louder.) As I came to my senses, I realized that the beep was coming from my kitchen stove as the power in my house was turning on and off. I ran into my kitchen to try and silence it. I wasn't exactly sure how I was going to do it, but I knew that I had to get some sleep. In the back of my mind, I was hoping that the guy from the electric company would just flip the switch. I staggered into the kitchen, but by this time, the power was off for good. No need to punch the stove! So, I went back to bed.

As the day went on, I realized something. Through this power outage, the Lord was trying to get my attention. He was wanting to teach me a lesson about His power. In fact, the revelation would fill much of my Sunday morning sermon. The message I was preaching on that Sunday happened to be "The Power of Praying in the Spirit." The congregation was getting fresh revelation!

The thing that the Holy Spirit was showing me was that there is a power outage in some of the body of Christ and He wants to restore it. He wants to "turn the power back on." To say the least, the lights have gone out and as a result many believers are walking around in the dark of diminished glory. They're making their journey with little or no light. Their lives are full of boredom and include little Holy Spirit activity (or ongoing dialogue with Jesus), stumbling and tripping over things on their paths.

> *"Jesus said to them… he who walks in the darkness does not know where he goes."*
>
> — John 12:35

They seek to turn the power back on but really, have no clue where to begin. They stagger in the dark, hoping that someone will just "flip the switch." Sad to say, many just give up and go back to bed. Nevertheless, I have good news! We don't have to return back to our place of slumber. With full confidence, we can get up and run to the One who is waiting to empower us with dynamite power. Don't go back to bed. Don't pull the covers over your head! I encourage you to shake off the dust and seek the Lord by praying in the Spirit. If you don't have the gift, ask Him for it. He so longs to bring you into His depository of power and love.

THE GREAT APOSTLE'S LANGUAGE

"I thank God, I speak in tongues more than you all..."

— 1 Corinthians 14:18 (NASB)

Who would have thought that the man who spoke most aggressively against God's people would end up being the one who would carry the most passion for them. Paul, the man who wrote over half of our New Testament, urges the (Corinth) church to pray in the Holy Spirit. Although Paul was never one to boast, he does give an "excited" glimpse of his prayer life. With a phrase like "I thank God, I speak in tongues more than you all" (1 Corinthians 14:18), I believe that he is attempting to prove the power of tongues. With this statement, I believe Paul prayed in the Spirit immensely. It was a high activity in the apostle's walk with the Lord. I can see him praying in tongues while riding his camel. I imagine him praying in tongues while writing letters to the churches, during his long ship rides from one region to another. This young apostle prayed in the Spirit excessively, and more than likely, he spoke in tongues during much of his day to day activity.

They had seen the power and ministry of Paul. He had become a written epistle for the church of Corinth to read (2 Corinthians 3:2, 3). Paul is now leading the church in amazing power and authority. I mean, he had turned whole cities upside down, healed the sick, established the church in love for Jesus (Acts 17:4-8). Seeing all of this, I can just imagine the church's eagerness to know the source of power. What has possessed this man? What causes him to enter cities with such boldness to demonstrate the gospel with signs and miracles, knowing that he may not make it out alive? What keep this young zealous follower of Jesus true to the high call of knowing Christ?

Paul was a man who ran hard and long in his calling. He ran the race set before him with such grace (2 Timothy 4:7). In view of this, I believe praying in the Spirit was a major contributing factor, keeping this apostle on course and faithful to the end. The gift of praying in tongues (excessively) kept the fire burning. With the glory of Christ as the flame, praying in tongues was the firewood. In the midst of immense persecution, with a fervent spirit he could say things like this:

> *"For I am already being poured out like a drink offering, and the time for my departure is near. I have fought the good fight, I have finished the race, I have kept the faith. Now there is in store for me the crown of righteousness, which the Lord, the righteous Judge, will award to me on that day—and not only to me, but also to all who have longed for his appearing."*
>
> *– 2 Timothy 4:6-8*

As they say, "the proof is in the pudding." I like to say it this way, "the proof is in the power". With an all-out display of powerful preaching (with signs and wonders) threading through Paul's life, it's no surprise that praying in the Spirit is closely linked to it. It's almost like Michael Jordan saying, "I practice more than any of my teammates." It would be difficult to argue that, since he was definitely the best of his time. Paul said that he prayed in the Spirit more than anyone, and when it came to preaching and converting whole regions and cities, he probably did more than anyone. There's just a clear correlation. In just one setting, Paul dismantled the long-established religion of pagan worship in Ephesus (see Acts 19). This tells me one thing - his heavenly prayer language was at fault. Unleashing his tongue to the prayer of the Spirit released his hands to the establishment of God's works.

LOST FOR WORDS

Jesus promised that when He ascended to the Father, the Holy Spirit would be sent to assist the disciples in their journey (John 14:26). Jesus called Him "the Helper." One definition of "help" is "to give or provide what is necessary to accomplish a task or satisfy a need; contribute strength or means to; render assistance to; cooperate effectively with; aid; assist." He would come into the believer's life, demonstrating and enacting the realm from which He came, heaven. The Holy Spirit would be and still is, heaven's Holy Ambassador. He helps shape our thoughts, form our words, and guide our steps. He is the smartest, wisest, and most sincere leader. He can take the things most powerful and make them utterly practical. Infinite in nature, He is beyond finite words. So, since we are limited in our feeble vocabulary, the Father thought it fit to send someone who would help resolve this very issue.

In Romans 8, Paul gives us insight to the Holy Spirit as our Helper. He introduces the Helper.

> *"Likewise the Spirit also helps in our weaknesses. For we do not know what we should pray as we ought, but the Spirit Himself makes intercession for us with groaning which cannot be uttered. Now He who searches the hearts knows what the mind of the Spirit is, because He makes intercession for the saints according to the will of God."*
>
> — Romans 8:26, 27

When we pray in the Spirit, He releases His language through us. We literally become the mouthpiece of heaven. When we are weak and at a loss for words, He prays through us the divine will of God.

Being the primary communicator of the Trinity, He loves to take the things unattainable and make them tangible. He is a specialist in taking the invisible and placing it right before our spiritual eyes. To Paul, He was the blinding light; to John, He was the One with burning eyes (Revelation 19:12).

When in drought, pray in the Spirit

There are times when I encounter something and I don't know how to pray. Most of the time, it's concerning a decision that I have to make. There are those times where deadlines are involved, people are waiting, and the pressure is on. One time in particular, I was selected to be a juror in a major court case. It was a lengthy case that took nearly 6 weeks and involved a lot of money. For weeks on end, we reviewed the same information over and over, and at various angles. Toward the four week mark, most of our heads were swimming with overloads of information. As for me, I was just trying to keep up. As we rounded the last week, the judge warned us that we should refresh our minds with the information given over the last few weeks, and ready ourselves to make a conclusive decision the next day. It was crunch time. To top it all off, they had selected me as the presiding (lead) juror. I was the one who would conduct the deliberation and lead the discussions in a way that drew a conclusion. The pressure was on. So on the way home that night, I drove the long way around and had a prayer meeting in my car. In desperation, I began to cry out for wisdom, praying in my understanding - asking for help according to the information we had been given. Before long, I became overwhelmed with the "informative" prayer. The tons of information were clouding my mind as I tried to connect with the Lord. I was praying from the head, not the heart. All of a sudden, I heard the Holy Spirit instruct me to pray in tongues. Immediately, I knew that this was a must. No longer would I try to "wrap my mind around the case," but I would simply yield my tongue to Him. So I did, and within the next few minutes I began to get downloads of wisdom on how I would conduct the deliberation, what amount I would aim for, and even the other jurors I was to pray for. By the time I got home, I felt confident in the coming decision and knew that the Lord had intervened. He became the lead advocate in this case! The next morning on the way to the courtroom, I continued to lean in and pray in the Spirit under my breath. As we entered the jury room to start deliberation, I could tell that the jury was leaning in a direction that I didn't see eye to eye with fully. However, within in a few minutes I felt the Holy Spirit break in to the room and release peace like a river. It wasn't long before we reached a verdict, and it went the way that the Holy Spirit had shown me.

As I tell my house of prayer crew, the Holy Spirit is the most talkative Person on the face of the planet. He is always speaking. Some would call Him a "chatter-box." However, the only difference in His talk and ours is this - every single word that He speaks carries the eternal weight of heaven. What He says and can say in a single syllable has the power to change all of our internal struggles. In a single moment, He can utterly silence our foes. He tells us to "be still and know that I am God" (Psalm 46:10) because He knows that if we will but slow down and just hear the mere and gentle whisper, we will be forever changed! He's not demanding that we hear the loud shouts of His voice, but the mere whisper will do. Why? Because His words carry weight and eternal value.

Think about this for a second. In the beginning, the earth was bare and without form. Some translations say that it was "void," empty of the creative design that we know today. With the Spirit hovering over the face of the earth (Genesis 1:2), God spoke. He didn't think about creating the universe, nor did He wave His hand in hopes something would happen… He spoke it. He said "Let there be light" and there was. Never has four words carried as much creative power as these did. In a short sentence, God Almighty created light. All of the things that cause light to be, happened in a mere moment. Now let's break it down a little more. As He said, "Let there be light", the first word alone was a most powerful truth. He said, "Let…!" In a single word, He allowed electrons and photons to form and give what we have now - glorious light. In a word, the Lord opened up the floodgates to all created design, and the light that emanates from Him was released onto the scene. All in the word "Let". Oh the power of His word.

This same God longs to pray through you and I. According to Paul (in Romans 8 and 1 Corinthians 14), the Holy Spirit carries a word for the believer, even when we're weak. We don't stand condemned when we're confused and at a loss for words. We are invited to loose our tongue for the Spirit to pray and intercede through us. And friends, it's not just a prayer filled with words, it's a word filled with creative power.

DIRECT COMMUNICATION WITH GOD

My son and I love the game of baseball. Ever since he was a little guy (around three years old), he's played for more than a dozen teams. We absolutely love it. It's such a game of skill and concentration, especially if you're a pitcher like my son. Standing on that mound, he understands that he must stay focused. With this concentration, comes the need for communication that is crucial between a coach, the catcher, and the guy on the mound (the pitcher). The three of us (coach, catcher, pitcher) have to communicate on pitch types (such as fastball, change up, curveball, etc...) before the game even begins. In doing so, we've established hand signals that only the three of us can understand.

The purpose of this is to keep the other team from knowing what we're doing. A certain number and location of my hand communicates where and how I want the pitch thrown. As coach, I'll usually sit down and communicate these signs to the catcher, who then signals to the pitcher. This method of hand and body communication is used all throughout the game. Another application is for batters and runners, communicating the kind of hit or run they should attempt. The purpose of this is to keep the other team guessing and off of their rhythm, as well as to communicate pitches, hits, and runs that the opposing team cannot intercept or understand. This keeps the game engaging and interesting. And I've learned that if players and coaches are communicating well, then the quality, effectiveness, and the team's performance increases dramatically.

> *"For one who speaks in a tongue*
> *does not speak to men but to God..."*
>
> – 1 Corinthians 14:2 (NASB)

The same goes true with praying in tongues. When we pray in the Spirit, we are directly communicating with God. With a straight line to the throne room, this channel of conversation is one that the enemy can't intercept. It's a "no-fly zone" for the enemy and his demons, a clear avenue for dialogue with no interference. It's my spirit straight to His, and His to mine. I've heard many people say, "Robby, when

I pray in tongues I don't know what I'm saying." And I usually reply, "That's the whole idea". In 1 Corinthians 14:14, Paul states, "For if I pray in a tongue, my spirit prays, but my mind is unfruitful." Much of the battle for the believer is in the high places of the mind, and the act of praying in the Spirit creates a "battle ground bypass". In a sense, we are unconsciously edifying ourselves. The Lord has a victory plan for your inner man and He wants to communicate it by the mode of praying in tongues, and it's a plan that the enemy can't translate and interfere with. I like to think of it as a "holy morse code."

The enemy doesn't intimately know our thoughts, only God does. However, he and his little demons hurl thoughts of accusation, doubt, fear, and anything that challenges the character and nature of God (Revelation 12:10). It is his aim to get us doubting God's goodness in our lives. Warring against this reality is the fight of much of our lives. However, friends, I have good news. We can rise above the playground of the enemy. We can soar above the place where our prayers are messed with and potentially intercepted. Although I love to pray in my understanding, there is still another dimension of prayer, and it's available to all who desire it.

PRAYING THE MYSTERIES OF GOD

"For one who speaks in a tongue does not speak to men but to God; for no one understands, but in his spirit he speaks mysteries."

— 1 Corinthians 14:2 (NASB)

Have you noticed the increase of TV shows and movies these days that are centered around mystery? Shows like CSI and NCIS (and many others) have come to dominate prime time television. Everything that happens in the events leading up to the end is in suspense, with a plot that is headed for a great crescendo. The truth is, mystery sells because people connect with it. It's part of our human makeup. We were made to search out mystery. It wasn't the world's idea, it's God's original design. Mystery was His idea!

Merriam Webster defines mystery as "a religious truth that one can know only by revelation and cannot fully understand," or "something not understood or beyond understanding." Strong's Concordance for mystery (mysterion) is "hidden thing, secret, not obvious to the understanding, a hidden purpose or counsel." It's spiritual and holy secrets, those God-purposes that haven't been revealed yet. It's interesting that the primary definition is centered around a spiritual reality. The veiled truth of something "religious."

We were made for mystery. We were designed to live with a "righteous tension and holy suspense." I've realized this more and more, especially when it comes to seeking the Lord in prayer and His word. Giving ourself to prayer and the word stirs our inward hunger like nothing else. Yet as we go deeper, we also realize our barrenness and necessity for Him. The more I learn about God, the more I realize how little I know about Him. The closer we get to Him, the bigger He appears and the smaller we seem.

JESUS AND PARABLES

When Jesus taught on the Kingdom of God, He would tell truths in the form of parables. He would say things like, "The Kingdom is like a treasure. The Kingdom is like a mustard seed," so on and so forth. He would relate His vast Kingdom to things that the hearer was familiar with.

What's great about a parable is that it doesn't disclose or reveal direct truth about something, as much as it helps one to discover the truth. It's about leading the hearer into a personal journey, only giving clues or hints to spur the hearer on to his or her own discovery. One Winn Griffin says, "A parable allows a person to put on another set of glasses and think. Truth, which is told and memorized, is quickly forgotten. Truth, which is discovered, will last a lifetime. The great value of parables is that they do not impose truth on a person; they place a person in a position to realize the truth." In other words, a parable was told not to reveal truth, but to hide it. The Lord reveals things for us, not from us. In the words of Ryan Atwood, Jesus wants His disciples to "wrestle with the text." He loves hiding Himself.

> *"These things (mysteries) Jesus spoke, and He went away and hid Himself from them."*
>
> *— John 12:36*

When my kids were just babies learning to walk, I loved to stand on the other side of the room and urge them to come to me. With eagerness in my eyes and joy in their reach, they stumbled across the room, because I was inducing their pursuit. Never did I scold them when they fell or stumbled, but rewarded them for their pursuit. They were trying and I loved their journey. In the same way, Jesus wants to induce pursuit. He wants to inventory the hungry and weed out the proud. He stands on the other side of these mysteries, urging us to keep up the pursuit. When He told parables, Jesus knew that knowledge is power and He didn't want the prideful to be powerful, so He hid His truths so that only the meek and committed could find the nuggets. I can imagine that Jesus loved looking out into the crowd to see His disciples scratching their heads.

> *"And the disciples came and said to Him, "Why do You speak to them in parables?" Jesus answered them, "To you it has been granted to know the mysteries of the kingdom of heaven, but to them it has not been granted. For whoever has, to him more shall be given, and he will have an abundance; but whoever does not have, even what he has shall be taken away from him. Therefore I speak to them in parables; because while seeing they do not see, and while hearing they do not hear, nor do they understand."*
>
> *– Matthew 10:10-13*

Just as we were made for mystery, so we were also made for discovery. This is why every kid loves hide and seek. The whole Christian journey is one of mystery and revelation. It's sort of like this - mystery leads to revelation, which leads to more revelation, leading to further mystery, which then leads back into revelation (Daniel 2:28). The point is that God just loves to lead His people into a place of perpetual searching and discovery. This is part of our created design. He sees it as glory!

> *"It is the glory of God to conceal a matter, but the glory of kings is to search out a matter."*
>
> *– Proverbs 25:2*

He is the endless ocean who is constantly revealing His depths. The moment you get to where your feet can touch, He reveals there is so much more room to step out. He continues to urge us on, "come on beloved, there's so much more! You think you've figured me out, but you've barely got your pinky toe wet. Just take another step and I will blow your mind." This is the beauty of God, that the ocean floor of His nature (His love, mercy, kindness, etc.) just keeps going!

In light of this, I believe that there are many, many discoveries to be made about God. In fact, the Christian life is exactly that - learning about God and learning how to relate to Him (John 17:3). Life is not about finding a good job or paying the bills, although those things are good. Friends, this journey is about discovering a Person. It's about peering into the eternal beauty and wisdom of the Godhead, to find Him and fall in love with Him. He will continue to wow our hearts and minds in order to keep us leaning into Him. This is the glory of mystery!

The Scriptures show us that we will forever be awestruck with His beauty as we continually discover His riches. For eons and eons, we will see the mysteries of God (His majesty, beauty, power, splendor, etc.) unfold before our very eyes. The glory of that great city will be attributed to this Man, and His glory will draw the nations. "Those who come from afar" will be an assembly of awestruck worshipers. Isaiah says it like this…

> *"Lift up your eyes and look about you: All assemble and come to you; your sons come from afar, and your daughters are carried on the hip. Then you will look and be radiant, your heart will throb and swell with joy; the wealth on the seas will be brought to you, to you the*

> riches of the nations will come. Herds of camels will cover your land, young camels of Midian and Ephah. And all from Sheba will come, bearing gold and incense and proclaiming the praise of the Lord."
>
> – Isaiah 60:4-6 (NIV)

In 1 Corinthians 14, Paul gives us a way to tap into these mysteries. He awakens the saints of Corinth, and declares that there are mysteries yet to be revealed. Mysteries that are far beyond anything they could ever imagine. And they're mysteries hidden for us, not from us. He makes mention of this chapters earlier.

> "Things which eye has not seen and ear has not heard, and which have not entered the heart of man, all that God has prepared for those who love Him."
>
> – 1 Corinthians 2:9 (NASB)

As a large city located in Greece, Corinth had inherently a very spiritual people. According to Hellenistic myth, the city was founded by a Greek god, so the Corinthians embraced the involvement of many gods. Much of their lives revolved around the acknowledgment and worship of these pagan gods. In other words, it was a culture saturated with a yearning for deep spiritual things (although it was a perverted form). Thus, we see Paul addressing a people interested in spiritual matters, in mysteries. While living in Corinth for 18 months (Acts 18:11), he learned of this deep yearning for the unknown, so he decided to tap into it by introducing the One who could fulfill this longing. Although their (past) pursuit of mystery and spirituality was sinful and carnal, Paul knew that their hunger would be fulfilled if they would tap into this gift of the Holy Spirit.

Even though some of our surroundings may not look the same as Corinth, the concept and reality are the same. Mankind is looking for deeper meaning and mystery that no one can comprehend. In the heart of every person is a longing cannot and will not go away. We are suckers for wonder.

Therefore, I encourage you to pray in the Spirit. For when we do, we're coming into contact with the mysteries of Christ - of His beauty and our identity in Him. When we pray in our heavenly language, we are putting ourselves in the path of encounter. We are asking for these mysteries to be revealed. I personally like to spend a majority of my secret place time by praying in the Spirit. Most of the time, I will open up my prayer time with subtle and short phrases that declare His beauty, followed by extensive time praying in tongues. And most of the time, it's not long before my heart is engaged. A majority of the revelations of God's beauty have come out of my secret place time of praying in the Spirit.

I urge you to connect with God's beauty by accessing this gift. He has secrets in His eternal plan that He longs to share with mankind and the gift of tongues is an invitation to enter into this eternal counsel. He wants lovers who have tapped into and know the depths and secrets of His heart.

> *"For one who speaks in a tongue does not speak to men but to God; for no one understands, but in his spirit he speaks mysteries."*
>
> – 1 Corinthians 14:2 (NASB)

Friends, speaking in tongues is a divine gift He has freely given, that we may continually discover the riches and depths of Christ. When we pray in our heavenly language, we are praying directly to God about God, and what He wants to do in the earth. In one language, we can learn simultaneous aspects of the Christian journey and as we've seen, there are multiple benefits. You don't have to live discouraged or dismayed. You can be on fire. You can burn with the same fire that's in His eyes (Revelation 1:14, 15), and you can burn with the desire that's in His heart. And I believe praying in the Spirit (in tongues) is one foundational key to do so.

I believe that lives filled with tongues will be hearts filled with the awe of His beauty. This gift is not something you have to strive for, buy, or even beg for. It's a gift that you receive. If you don't currently have this gift, I encourage you to slow down and ask Him for this gift. Ask Him for grace to enter into this divine gift of praying in tongues. You may not receive it right away. It's different for every person. However, with a heart of rest, continue to press into this gift. It will change your life - forever!

> *"Is anyone thirsty? Come and drink— even if you have no money! Come, take your choice of wine or milk— it's all free!"*
>
> — Isaiah 55:1 (NLT)

eight

My House Shall Be Called

It's one of my favorite stories. The scene is in Jerusalem (on Passover) and Jesus enters the temple to do business in the very city in which His return was centered around (Matthew 21). Most of the Jews had read the passages prophesying that the Messiah would return to save and deliver the people from their oppressor. He would be declared the coming Governor in Micah 5:2, the Prince of peace in Isaiah 9:6, and quite frankly, the Ruler and King who would crush the oppressor (Isaiah 9:4). This Messiah was coming and His very kingdom would come with Him. For a Jew under immense control and ungodly oppression, this is great news.

So we have at the climax of Rome's oppressive rule and brutal oversight, a great anticipation of a coming King to the holy city. What would He look like? Would He wear a kingly robe? Would He fight with a sword and ride on a chariot? Many questions, I'm sure, filled this Jewish community. Matthew 21:10 declares this very plainly, "When He had come into Jerusalem, all the city was moved, saying, Who is this?" Sounds like David and his men when bringing the ark back into Jerusalem (Psalm 24:7).

In this context, Jesus rides into the beloved city on a colt, with the donkey accompanying it. He is doing this to fulfill what had been spoken by Isaiah and Zechariah (9:9). Wait a minute. You mean the King of kings is riding on a colt, not a bold stallion or a flaming chariot? Jesus actually picked the meeker and smaller one - the colt. Jesus has a key moment to show off big and bring the fireworks, and He chooses to coast in on an animal barely able to find it's own way. Oh the beautiful irony of the gospel!

I can only imagine the excitement and anticipation. The very One whom generations had longed and waited for. He was here! The promise which had been held back like waters before a dam, was right before them. This moment hinged on a Man, and He was here! He was entering into the very context in which He promised He would deliver the people from. Isaiah's words were fresh in their minds and hearts - "Behold, this is our God for whom we have waited that He might save us. This is the LORD for whom we have waited; Let us rejoice and be glad in His salvation" (Isaiah 25:9).

In their excitement, the people break out into praise (Matthew 21:9). The scene very quickly turns into a corporate worship service. It's such an intense moment that the participants start cutting branches off of trees so they can express their gratitude and bubbling excitement. One translation says "An exceptionally large crowd gathered and carpeted the road before him with their cloaks and prayer shawls. Others cut down branches from trees to spread in his path" (Passion Translation). The worshipping community paved the road with their praise and prayer!

To the worshipping crowd, the age old prophecies were being fulfilled before their very eyes. The stories they had heard from their ancestors of a coming Man who would save the world, this was the moment. And they were just feet away watching it all unfold. There was no better time to rejoice. What an amazing experience that had to be!

As the praise and worship continues, Jesus enters the city. The anticipation grows and grows among the worshipping community. Where will He go? What will He do? Most anyone would have made an immediate trip to the city's most influential (person of peace). Maybe even a stop by the local restaurant or hometown bookstore to connect with the city's noblemen. Yet, Scripture tells us that the Son of Man wept over the city for a moment and then went straight to the temple - to the heart of the city (Mark 11:15-17; Luke 19:45-46). You see, the temple was a place cherished by all of Jewish forefathers and the existing people group. It was the crown of the community, the diamond in the land. The temple was their treasure. For decades, the people of Israel and Judah had fought and given up their lives for this very place. It was the dwelling place of God. It was the house of prayer. Well, at least that was God's original intent.

With a clear mission, God's own begotten Son marches into the beloved temple and drives out all who were selling and doing business. The temple, originally designed for encounter with the Holy One, had now become a place for profit and gain. You could say it had become a "non-prophet" ministry. A place that was set apart for man to enjoy God and God to enjoy man, had become a place of heavy yoke and oppression to the visiting community. In light of this, Jesus wreaks "holy havoc" on what was hindering the mission of the temple (aka the house of prayer).

> *"And Jesus entered the temple and drove out all those who were buying and selling in the temple, and overturned the tables of the money changers and the seats of those who were selling doves."*
>
> *– Matthew 21:12*

Quoting prophecy from both Isaiah (56:7) and Jeremiah (7:9, 10), Jesus declares this truth with such precision.

> *"And He said to them, It is written, My house shall be called a house of prayer; but you are making it a robbers' den."*
>
> *– Matthew 21:13*

Just verses earlier, it says that as Jesus entered, the city was shaken. His very presence caused a city to quake in reverence and fear. How many of us can say that our presence does that? This Man from Nazareth had everyone's attention. He had summoned the hearts of men and was shaking all that could be shaken, to declare this powerful truth - "My Daddy's house (dwelling) is a place of prayer." It is a place of divine fellowship and conversation between man and God. It's where human beings talk to God and He talks to them. In essence He is saying, this is My mission for the temple and it should be yours as well. It was a time for a holy audit from the Man Himself as He is calling divine order back into the system of the temple. Heaven's ambassador had stepped into the building to call forth a most righteous board meeting. What didn't belong in the quarters of prayer and worship, was cast out by the Son of Man.

When Jesus "cracked the whip" in the temple, He wasn't declaring the exterior name on a building. He wasn't implying that we should simply name our ministries or churches by "house of prayer." He was stating His intention and identity on the body of Christ. Speaking to the heart, He was referring to the inward expression of prayer, where all ministry comes out of the place of prayer. It was to be a place of heaven and earth exchange, where a people were defined and shaped in intimacy. This is the house that God intends to build. Not a house of programs or profit, but a house of prayer. A culture of prayer… This is the Father's house!

I believe that the Lord is once again bringing order back into His house. In a sense, He is marching back into His congregation to declare that His house shall be a place of prayer - a center of worship and encounter. He wants conversation with His people. It's not that Jesus is in a bad mood or wants to pick a fight. It's just that His Father has an eternal purpose for His people and the Son is adamant about guarding that. The Son has an eternal inheritance that He died for and will return for one whose eyes are focused like His. As my friend Travis once said, "He's going to get what He wants, not because He's a brat, but because He's a good Son and belongs to a good Father". He will do anything to keep that inheritance true to its purpose.

"Lord, you alone are my inheritance, my cup of blessing. You guard all that is mine."

– Psalm 16:5 (NLT)

Another interesting thing about this account is that which follows. After Jesus cleanses the temple, He begins another cleansing process. He begins healing the blind and the lame (Matthew 21:14). In front of the onlooking crowd, Jesus begins to openly destroy the works of the devil. In one setting, two different groups of people were moved. One by His strong hand of authority and the other by His compassionate heart of mercy. This tells us that Jesus will do whatever it takes to keep the mission clear. He will either run the wicked out or draw the broken near.

It's crucial to see that being the house of prayer creates a context for Kingdom power to come forth. The call to prayer is coupled with the call to power.

> "And the blind and the lame came to Him in the temple, and He healed them. But when the chief priests and the scribes saw the wonderful things that He had done, and the children who were shouting in the temple, "Hosanna to the Son of David," they became indignant and said to Him, "Do You hear what these children are saying?" And Jesus *said to them, "Yes; have you never read, 'Out of the mouth of infants and nursing babies You have prepared praise for Yourself'?"
>
> – Matthew 21:14-16

HIS NAME WILL BE GREAT

Just before the ending of the Old Testament, we have a young prophet prophesying several key ingredients in the Lord's coming, related to both the first and second coming of Christ. It's the spirit of Elijah prophecy, where the Lord promises to turn the hearts of the fathers to the children and the children to their fathers (Malachi 4:5, 6).

Another key prophecy is in chapter one, where the Lord is addressing the priests. They no longer honor the name of the Lord, and He is confronting their defilement. They are perverting the order of worship they were called to by kindling "strange fire" on the altar. Malachi says, "Oh that there were one among you who would shut the gates, that you might not uselessly kindle fire on My altar! I am not pleased with you, says the Lord of hosts, nor will I accept an offering from you" (Malachi 1:10).

Just after He says this, the Lord drops a bomb in their laps, saying, "For from the rising of the sun even to its setting, My name will be great among the nations, and in every place incense is going to be offered to My name, and the grain offering that is pure; for My name will be great among the nations" (1:11). The Lord declares that His name will get the honor it's due "where incense and pure grain is offered" to Him. In essence, He is saying that His name will be glorified where altars to Him are established. Comprised of different ingredients (Exodus 30:34) incense was offered in the Holy Place of Moses' tabernacle (Hebrews 9:3, 4). It was to be offered up perpetually by the priests (Exodus 30:8). Incense signified the ingredients of His New Testament priests. Grain signified pure and yielded lives. Both ingredients were a prophetic picture of the "smoke" of our yielded lives ascending to His throne as worship.

Our identity and privilege as priests are manifest as we offer up our lives by prayer, intercessions, and worship.

> *"May my prayer be counted as incense before You; the lifting up of my hands as the evening offering."*
>
> — Psalm 141:2 (NASB)

The Lord desires to make His name known across the earth. From Asia to America, Jesus longs to make His name famous. It has always been the Father's primary goal. And He will do it by and through His praying and worshipping church. As Malachi points out, our devotion expressed in prayer (intercession and worship) marks the spot for His name to be established and known. We see this is what took place in the early church...

> *"They were continually devoting themselves to the apostles' teaching and to fellowship, to the breaking of bread and to **prayer**. Everyone kept feeling a sense of awe (honor for the name of God)..."*
>
> — Acts 2:42, 43 (NASB)

> *"...fear fell upon them all and the name of the Lord Jesus was being magnified."*
>
> — Acts 19:17b (NASB)

One of the defining reasons that He is raising up the praying church in this hour is because He wants His name to have complete influence in all nations (Matthew 24:14). Statistics show us that houses (and ministries) of prayer are popping up all over the globe. From the corners of African villages to the plains of Montana, He is divinely orchestrating an end-time prayer movement that will usher in the greatness of His name. The incense of worship and intercession is arising across the earth, and I believe that the cry of this generation of believers will sound like the early church - "we will devote ourselves to prayer and to the ministry of the word" (Acts 6:4). He is building His house of prayer (Psalm 127:1), and is asking that we partner with Him.

Just as He urged Aaron and the Levites to keep the flame going (Leviticus 6:13), the Lord is calling this generation to do the same. He says to us, "Don't let the fire on the altar go out. Continue to offer up your life with prayers, intercessions, and worship as the incense before My throne." He's now asking His church to host more prayer meetings than board meetings; more sacred assemblies than potlucks. He's raising up those like David who will host altars of worship and prayer, simply because He wants to bring whole cities and nations into the power of His name.

There is a deep longing in this generation that goes beyond just doing something. We want to be something. Friends, we can answer this longing. We can become the house of prayer. Our lives were designed to burn and release the incense of heaven before God. May we offer the worship and prayer (incense) that He is due.

WE SHALL BE A HOUSE OF PRAYER

He is raising up cultures of prayer across the earth. I believe this will be one of the signs of the times, when He restores His bride to the place of wholehearted love. Operating in full agreement for His return, the Spirit and the bride say "come" (Revelation 22:17). In order to see a worship and prayer movement established and sustained, it's going to take individuals going deep in the lifestyle of prayer, worship, and the commitment to obey. Before this thing becomes a vast corporate expression, it must first be a personal reality and an inward embracing. All of our public expression must be an overflow of our personal and secret place.

> *Cities will be overcome by the presence of God when individuals are overshadowed by it.*

When the Lord wants to do something outwardly, He always begins inwardly. He will begin to work in the deep recesses of men's hearts to see it manifest in realms of society. We see this in the life of Moses, where the Lord took him alone to the mountain to deal with him as the shepherd. He ministered to David in the fields of Bethlehem. The man after God's heart was shaped in those fields. He was trained to reign well before he took the keys of the Kingdom. Nehemiah wept bitterly inside his prayer closet before he laid the first stone. John the Baptist was tucked away in the wilderness years before he became a public voice. We could go on and on with how the Lord establishes things first on the inside of a man before He does on the outside. It's just how He does things!

This is what He wants to do with the prayer movement. He's not so much concerned with building another ministry or venue. Rather, He is much more devoted to making us a house of prayer. Personally, I have experienced this firsthand. My passion to build the house of prayer always corresponds with my vision to be a house of prayer. Simply stated, how can I expect to lead others to a life of prayer if I am not doing it myself.

The cleansing of merchants and robbers is a prophetic picture of what He wants to do on the inside of His people. He wants to rid the house of anything that doesn't belong. My wife can walk in our house and know immediately if anything is out of place. She can spot when something has been moved or tampered with. Why? Because she's passionate about her house. It belongs to her and she likes it clean and tidy. It's just the way she's set up. Same way with the Lord. He is particular and passionate about His house. As His possession, He knows right away if you've been tampered with, abused, and even adjusted by someone else. He has a certain way He wants things set up on the inside of His church and doesn't mind stirring things up in order to get it back the way He wants it.

I feel like much of the shaking that's coming in days ahead, is Jesus Himself marching into the temple to overturn the tables of our inward chambers. He wants to shake our interior, that He may shake every realm of society. This is His lovely discipline. He doesn't do it to harm us or to cause us to draw back. Beloved, He does it because He wants a house unhindered and engaged with what He's saying and doing. He wants your heart to be fully His. He wants heaven on earth and will flip a few tables to see it come about. He just won't settle for anything less than that!

As Bill Johnson once said, "He will often offend the mind to reveal our hearts." This is why He disciplined each of the seven churches in the book of Revelation. He wanted them to hear "what the Spirit is saying to the church" (Revelation 3:22). He will walk into the house and say things like, "That doubt doesn't belong here. Is that

For the glory of the Lord to cover the earth, it is crucial that it covers our prayer times.

offense? O we have to remove that. Fear, where did you come from? You must go! Lust, who said you could enter My abode?" I think you get the idea. His tender love is often manifest in firm discipline. Whatever it looks like, He is determined to have a house clean and ready to receive the things necessary to make us His house of prayer (Ephesians 5:27). He, the Master Builder, wants conversation with His people once again, and He's determined to get it.

nine

Practicality of Prayer

I am a guy who embraces the practicalities of life. Whether I'm praying, preaching, prophesying, playing with my children, or hammering a nail, I want to know if there is a more effective and enjoyable way to do so. I believe everyone would agree with me on that one. I've come to realize that God is practical as well as powerful. He is a Father who gives us the most simple and clear instruction, then soon backs it up with supernatural power (signs and wonders). He gives us clear boundaries and then instructs us to explore the countryside. In other words, the practicals can often be gateways to experience the powerful. They just work together.

At one time, I thought a vibrant prayer life was for those who were "hyper-spiritual" and a little strange in their social skills. It made sense that the heroes of the faith possessed such vibrant prayer lives, but I never understood that I could have the same. I imagined I needed to be a certain spiritual status to have a prayer life, and I soon found out that this just isn't true. Whether you're a stay at

> *Whether you're a stay at home mom, a teacher, preacher, janitor, or doctor, developing a prayer life is for anyone wanting to draw closer to God.*

home mom, a teacher, preacher, janitor, or doctor, developing a prayer life is for anyone wanting to draw closer to God. There is no pre-qualification process aside from being washed in the blood of Jesus. If you are a believer, prayer is for you.

However, as growing more and more in prayer, I've realized that prayer is the most practical and natural thing we could do. It is for everyone, "weird or normal," and I believe there are key practical ways that will help you to grab hold of this thing for yourself. These simple and practical keys have helped me tremendously in my journey. Being intentional in them has helped me gain momentum in my pursuit of God. Here are some things I have adopted.

PRAYER SCHEDULE

As followers of Christ, I believe it's imperative that we create opportunities to encounter Him, not only wait for them to happen. The Lord wants a people postured to receive Him in every situation of life. We see several men in Scripture who lived in this postured state. Daniel prayed three times a day and David praised the Lord seven times a day.

> *"Seven times a day I praise You, because of Your righteous ordinances."*
>
> – Psalm 119:164

> *"...he (Daniel) entered his house (now in his roof chamber he had windows open toward Jerusalem); and he continued kneeling on his knees three times a day, praying and giving thanks before his God, as he had been doing previously."*
>
> – Daniel 6:10

Their journey of loving God was directly connected to their practical and frequent commitment. They didn't just wait for encounters to happen, they grabbed ahold of God with intentional practicality and lived from encounter. As men of deep commitment to the Lord, they obviously saw the necessity of consecrating their devotion times to the Lord. Remember, God gave us appointed times and seasons in creating the cosmos. He didn't just spin the globe and hope that everything would work out. He strategically formed all the stars, moons, and planets with grave intentionality. Even when He desired to meet with Israel, He appointed special times and convocations. The Hebrew word for "convocations" is miqra, meaning, "calling together or sacred assembly." The Lord of heaven was calling His people to set apart and consecrate a time when they would meet and celebrate. It was a scheduled time.

> *"Speak to the sons of Israel and say to them, 'The Lord's appointed times which you shall proclaim as holy convocations–My appointed times are these."*
>
> – Leviticus 23:2

When you establish a prayer schedule, you are setting up private meetings with the King of the all the earth. This kind of perspective brings a sobriety. Imagine you received an invitation to meet the President of the United States at the White House on a certain day at a certain time. In the invitation, there are no rules of arriving on time or being punctual. However, I think that anyone receiving the invitation would know that it's expected of them to arrive on time. It's just what one should because this is the President - the commander and chief of the most powerful army on the earth.

For me personally, the best time for focused prayer is in the morning while everything is still fairly quiet. I choose to awaken the day instead of it awakening me. However, I have friends who prefer to have their secret place time later at night, after everyone is in bed. Others may prefer to have theirs in the mid-afternoon. Nevertheless, whatever time you decide to set apart in your schedule, consistency is the key. Find what time works for you and jump in with commitment and frequency.

PRAYER LIST

Often times in prayer, so many things are pulling at our attention. Either our phone is going off like a fire engine, texts are coming in like planes on a runway, or the to-do list is screaming our name. Whatever the case, it's important to understand that when you decide to take up the occupation of prayer and make it your first priority, the potential distractions will only increase. Facebook will all of a sudden notify you. That family member you haven't talked to for years and even decades, finally calls. The friend whom you haven't seen in years, finally decides to drop in. The list of distractions goes on and on. In fact, I often say to anyone starting a life in prayer, don't be surprised when you encounter distractions, but rather be surprised if you don't immediately come face to face with them. Pressing into the Lord surely invites immediate resistance. This is one sure principle found in the word of God and the life of every aggressive believer.

So why a prayer list? A prayer list helps keep you focused on the task at hand. I've heard it from several sources that praying with a prayer list will increase your prayer life 6 to 10 times. For example, if you currently pray five minutes a day, with a prayer list you will more than likely pray thirty to fifty minutes instead. Many of us make "to-do" lists to keep us focused on the needed tasks, so how much more should we adopt a prayer list to keep us focused on our time before the Lord.

Just like many of our jobs require objectives or goals, so prayer lists work the same way. Whether you're targeting that lost loved one, a job promotion, praying through Psalms, or just praying general prayers, I believe prayer lists will help keep you focused and engaged.

If you are new to this prayer list thing, start simple. Below is an example of starting simple and creating something that is "doable". Start with 3 points.

1. Prayer **related to God**

    a. Declare the knowledge of God. Pray and speak out His greatness and the beauty of His Son.

    Example : Psalm 145

    b. Ask the Holy Spirit to give you deeper understanding of who God is. He wants to enlighten you more than you want to be enlightened.

    Example: Ephesians 1:17, 18

2. Prayer **related to people**

    a. Ask for grace to walk in relationship with others around you - empowered in the second commandment.

    Example: Romans 12:10

    b. Ask for lost ones to be brought into the Kingdom, by preaching and declaring the name of Jesus.

    Example: Titus 2:11

3. Prayer **related to yourself**

    a. Ask for deeper understanding of the word and a spirit of wisdom and revelation as you read and meditate on the Scriptures.

    Example: Psalm 119:18

    b. Ask that you would be strengthened in your identity in Christ, and empowered to obey.

    Example: Colossians 1:9-14

In saying this, don't feel that you have to stay "glued" to the list, but allow yourself to flow in the place of prayer. There will be times when you're sticking to the list and all of a sudden, out of nowhere, the Holy Spirit begins to emphasize a particular phrase or passage, person or topic. I encourage you to live in that moment and stay in the river as long as you feel led. Don't feel that you have to jump back into the next prayer topic. If you do, you're missing the whole point. Again, remember that a prayer list is to provide opportunity for encounters, that we may stay engaged and focused on the real task at hand - encountering the heart God. May we never rejoice in our discipline of prayer, but only use it as a tool in our pursuit of encounter.

BE FAITHFUL

This one has some heavy weight on it. It's what separates the men from the boys. Joyce Meyer once said, "Faithfulness is not doing something right once but doing something right over and over and over and over." Simple yet so true. If you're ever going to have a vibrant prayer life, you must embrace faithfulness.

I believe that faithfulness produces fruitfulness. Remember David. It was those long days in the fields of Bethlehem that prepared him for the throne of Jerusalem. It was the training ground in being a man after God. In addressing Moses, the Lord even calls Himself the Lord who is "abounding in… faithfulness" (Exodus 34:6). This is a recurring theme in the character of God throughout Scripture, that He is faithful to each generation. The psalmist boasts that He is "faithful in all that He does" (Psalm 33:4).

The Bible calls us priests and kings unto our God (Revelation 1:5, 6) and Proverbs 20:28 declares "Unfailing love and faithfulness protect the king; his throne is made secure through love." There is great safety and refuge in being faithful - bringing protection to our kingly calling in Christ. It provides a safeguard in seasons of success as well as seasons of testing. Our faithfulness to show up (even when we don't feel like it) will inevitably create context for Him to.

As you adopt a prayer life, there will be days when you just don't want to pray. You'll think of ten other things you could or should be doing. You will inevitably encounter emotions of dread, dismay, and just plain boredom. I say these things because many people aren't aware of these emotions and when they feel them, they start doubting the sincerity of their prayer life, and many times give up. Understand that these emotions are normal. It's not about whether you encounter these feelings, but rather how you respond when you do. There will be those seasons when prayer is among the last of things you want to be doing. But, it's in those times that determines your destination. This principle is clear throughout Scripture. Those who rise above faint emotions to embrace their calling and convictions, will be given authority and a heightened capacity to know Him.

I've heard it many times that love is commitment. I believe that's why the Lord doesn't want man to be alone. He wants man to experience the dynamics of faithfulness and commitment, especially when it's not convenient or easy. It is probably the greatest trainer in the arena of life.

We should live in such a way that the generation after us finds great momentum to keep running. We should be building the next generation a platform of faithfulness. As a fruit of the Spirit, it is one of the greatest commodities in the Kingdom of God (Galatians 5:22). Mother Teresa once said "I do not ask for success, I ask for faithfulness." She knew that when her compassion married faithfulness, she would have a powerful and life-giving combination.

The Lord is not asking that we have it all figured out. He's just urging us to stick it out. As the old saying goes, "If you don't quit, you win." This is especially true when developing a life of prayer. There will be days when you are fighting to find the words to say, the thoughts to meditate on, and the Scripture to pray. On the other hand, there will be those days when you feel that everything is just clicking, that the words you are speaking are straight from the mouth of God. You will experience both bitter and sweet realities in prayer. With this range of emotions, it is important that we gain a long term vision for this thing. Don't give up, keep praying!

Streams and rivers aren't formed by one big burst of rushing water. Rather, they're formed by the continual and trickle from small streams. It's called erosion. We must learn to "erode" in our prayer time. Sometimes we will see immediate breakthrough and other times it may take time to chip away at that mountain. However, we must understand that He hears and we will see breakthrough in His timing. In fact, every time we don't see the immediate's, that is a greater reason to draw back into the secret place of prayer. Remember, the greatest secret in the Kingdom is the secret place. Every time you sow into the secret place, you are casting seed. In time, that seed will take form and create context for a life of breakthrough.

In light of this, I want to encourage you to go ahead and take the pressure off. Realize that you are going to have challenging days of prayer. Realize that there are various dynamics and emotions involved when you decide to cultivate a life of prayer. It's not going to look like your friend's journey, nor should it. Take a deep breath and develop your own. Realize that this thing is a journey. Go ahead, laugh, and learn to lean into the grace given by the Holy Spirit. Besides, without Him we have no hope of developing any type of prayer life. Without His leadership in this thing, we are just throwing words into the air.

Learn to gauge your prayer life over longer periods of time instead of one day, one week, or even one month. I have learned to inventory my life in God by months and even years. Instead of focusing on those momentary successes or even mess-ups, I like to step back and see the panoramic view of my journey. It's a wise way to number our days.

PRAY DAILY

I have a firm rule in my own life that guards me from living in apathy. I use the acronym **D-A-Y**. It goes like this:

Daily pray and partake of the word. The two (word and prayer) go together. They are the "perfect storm" of the believer's life. In the midst of much busyness and increasing activity, the early church committed themselves to the place of prayer and ministry of the word (Acts 6:4). To remain sharp in our spirit, we must make the commitment to never let a day go by that we don't engage in the word and in prayer. It's the safeguard against spiritual dullness. History in prayer creates breakthrough for the future. Make your days a seedbed of prayer, where you're constantly sowing faith and promise into its soil.

Ask the Holy Spirit to open and enlighten your eyes. Simply reading the word and saying prayers won't keep us from boredom. We must have the spirit of revelation (Ephesians 1:17, 18). We must learn from the great teacher Himself. I always lead my prayer and devotional times with a simple prayer of help from the Holy Spirit. Ask that He open your eyes to the majesty of dialoguing with God. Many can listen, but few actually hear.

Yield to what He is saying. This is where the rubber meets the road. James exhorts us to "do" the word. He urges the believer to act on what he / she hears. It's not enough for a quarterback to read the playbook, he must "do" the play. He must engage his fellow team members with what is written. We have the living word in our possession and the question is, who will actually hear, obey, and do the word.

Don't wait for the trials and hardships to hit before you run to God in prayer. Go ahead and put it in action. That way when hardships do come, you will already be positioned and grounded to take the punch.

DEVELOP FRIENDSHIPS TO COMPLEMENT YOUR JOURNEY

Now this is a heavy one. Engaging in fellowship with others who are embracing a life of prayer is vitally important. In my opinion, it's probably top two or three of what either catapults or hinders many in their journey of developing a vibrant devotion life. Much of the weight of our journey is in our friendships and relationships.

Elijah had Elisha, Moses had Joshua, Paul had Timothy, and Jesus had His disciples. Don't you just love how God in flesh modeled this truth of developing friendships. He very well could have chosen to do His own thing all alone, but He chose to pick friends with whom He would partner with. I call this building "kindred fire." It's developing Holy Ghost friendships. I'm not talking about someone who is a "yes man" or someone who is just like you, but a friend who shares the simple core values of the Kingdom. Someone who is focused on the pursuit of God in His word, in prayer, and embraces radical obedience. This type of template in any friendship is always a sure way to sharpen the iron of your resolve.

Jesus never sent His disciples out by themselves. Rather, He commissioned them as a two-man army. In Luke 10:1, Jesus sent the 72 disciples out two by two, making up 36 groups of world changers. They were the "eager beavers" of the Kingdom. These men were the very ones who would run ahead of Him and represent His Kingdom, demonstrated by acts of service and signs and wonders. It's amazing that the Son of God would commission them to go ahead of Him. Talk about trust! I personally believe that Jesus realized He had poured into them to point that if one got "off track" or diverted, the other would be there to help rein him back in.

Jesus was a man of trust. It's ironic that the very man He appointed as treasurer was the one who would betray Him for money. The one He entrusted to hold the money bag is the very one who would hand Him over. Because He valued partnership, He entrusted His boys with the gospel. He desired ambassadors of the Kingdom and what better way to pull this off, than to employ weak and broken individuals. O, the beauty of the gospel.

Many of us are desiring to have an immovable and "iron resolve," and much of the iron resolve that God will develop in us is found in us embracing friendships with those who are desiring the same values.

> *"Iron sharpens iron, so one man sharpens another."*
>
> *— Proverbs 27:17*

READ BOOKS AND RESOURCES ON PRAYER

In studying on prayer throughout the years, I have found one thing to be true. Every great revival was first founded by prayer. In the many chronicles of revivals out there, you will always see the foot prints of prayer in its pages. Most fires began with one man or woman who threw him or herself before the Lord in passionate prayer. Reading these accounts of the outbreaks of prayer will stir your heart to reach for more in the place of prayer.

I remember one of the first books I ever read on revival was a book called "Holy Spirit Revivals" by Charles Finney. It was a book that chronicled the young man's life of ministry and his experience in the Holy Spirit. I recall reading accounts of how Mr. Finney employed full-time intercessors to travel with him as he preached the gospel. They were hired to literally bombard the heavens in intercession. These two men would go in days before Finney was to preach, and they would begin to tear down strongholds in the area - by fervent prayer, fasting, and intercession. Once they felt that the air was clear, Finney would then preach. Under the power of the Holy Spirit, bars would shut down, drug lords would get saved, the sick would get healed, the blind eyes would be opened, etc. In other words, heaven would sit down in that city in response to "revival prayer."

Once my young eyes read these stories and accounts of how God used these ordinary men and women, I was forever ruined. The words on these pages had now become the cry of my heart. I now frequent my reading with accounts on prayer - especially the classics, like E.M. Bounds, Charles Finney, D.L. Moody, Charles Spurgeon, etc. I believe if we want to see what the fathers and mothers in the faith saw, we have to believe like they believed and pray with the same intense faith that they prayed with. These books and resources are great tools to calibrate our hearts and ultimately, give us vision for more.

Some great authors on prayer include E.M. Bounds, Charles Spurgeon, Brother Lawrence, Charles Finney, Bob Sorge, Mike Bickle, and Cory Russell.

Some great "must-reads" include "Secrets of the Secret Place" by Bob Sorge and "Complete Works of E.M. Bounds" by E.M. Bounds.

COMBINE FASTING WITH PRAYER

In the Sermon on the Mount, Jesus exhorted His disciples to fast (Matthew 6:16-18). Coupled with this, was the call to pray and give. The Son of Man knew the way to a refreshed heart was by an empty stomach. As Bill Johnson states, "in the natural we satisfy hunger by feasting, but in the Kingdom we satisfy hunger by fasting". Simply said, many of our encounters with the Lord are waiting behind "denied indulgences", by fasting and prayer.

Historical accounts show us that the early church fasted 2 days a week. Their sending was coupled with prayer and fasting (Acts 13:2, 3), and they knew the way to remain faithful to Jesus and the message, was to push back the plate. In doing so, they pulled themselves up to the table of the Lord. It was Daniel who fasted and saw angelic visitation with breakthrough (Daniel 10), Esther fasted and prayed for the breakthrough of her peoples impending judgment (Esther 4:16), the establishment of elders in the early church was accompanied by it (Acts 14:23), God called His people to divert impending danger through fasting with prayer (Joel 1:14; 2:12), and it was Anna who anticipated the coming of the Lord with fasting and prayer (Luke 2:37).

Jesus plainly tells us that fasting with prayer introduces breakthrough that we would've otherwise missed (Matthew 17:21). It's not about earning, rather, it's about yearning. We earn nothing by fasting, rather we position our hearts and minds to receive that which is already available in Him. Whether it is personal or corporate, God loves to release revival in the context of prayer and fasting.

"Prayer and fasting are the power twins of the Kingdom."

– Dave Roberson

DEVELOP YOUR OWN "SECRET PLACE"

Having your own place to pray and get alone is an absolute must. I firmly believe that one can pray anywhere, yet I've found that there is something scared about designating a place to get away from the noise and clutter of the day. For me, I have two places where I seem to almost automatically connect with the Lord, my home office and the One27 Prayer Room. Both of these places are personal sanctuaries that are set up with minimal distractions, and I have come to know both of these places as my "slow-down" rooms. As I have cultivated both places with much prayer and worship, it's almost without even noticing that I run to these places as points of refuge. They have now become places of delight and "hot spots" of my devotional time.

There are a few ways to make these places more enjoyable…

i. First, I like having a place that has very little traffic. For example, using the living room as your designated place may be a little tough. It's where most people hang out. When Jesus used the term "prayer closet," He was making a point. Not necessarily that believers have to use a literal closet (where you store your wardrobe), but rather He was signifying a place that was solitude. There's no traffic in a closet.

ii. Secondly, I like to set the atmosphere with music and good lighting. We are musical beings who love to make melodies and tone, and I always engage better when I pray along with music. Adding (anointed and Holy Spirit inspired) music to the secret place enhances the experience.

iii. Thirdly, pick a designated place that has enough room to move around. For me, being able to pace and pray is a huge plus. It allows me to get my mind and heart going with my body. And apart from that, I'm just hyper by nature. I can't sit still for too long. I want to move in prayer!

UNDERSTAND THAT PRAYER IS TO BE ENJOYABLE

"Even those I will bring to My holy mountain and make them joyful in My house of prayer."

— Isaiah 56:7 (NASB)

Here are some simple and practical ways to make your prayer time more enjoyable…

I. **DEVELOP THE KNOWLEDGE OF GOD**

The life of joy for believers must be rooted and grounded in the knowledge of God and the beautiful truth that He delights in and desires me. This reality will set our inner man ablaze as we seek to delight in Him. We can only become a people after God's own heart when we understand that He is after ours.

Understanding that God is a just and rewarding master and owner is the key to joyful stewardship. The servant with one talent had a wrong view of his master and it determined how he sowed his talents, abilities, and what had been given him (Matthew 25:24, 25). Instead of sowing with joy, he "hoarded" with fear. So when searching for God, don't think about how much YOU love Him, simply think about how much HE loves you! His love will draw us to that place of deeper devotion.

Saying and praying the wonderful attributes of God in your prayer time will help in engaging your heart with Him. I like to mingle my whole day with thoughts of His greatness. It keeps me in the spirit of prayer and thankfulness.

II. **PRAY WITH MUSIC**

We are musical beings, where our hearts come alive with melodies and tone. Music causes our mind and heart to open up to the environment we are in. The mystery of music is in the being of God. God is a musician. The Holy Spirit is a musical Spirit. Music is the greatest form of entertainment in every culture. Why? Because the human spirit is musical. Music helps stir the ability to hear and perceive. Elijah said it like this:

> *"But now bring me a minstrel. And it came about, when the minstrel played, that the hand of the Lord came upon Him."*
>
> *– 2 Kings 3:15*

The power of music is amazing. The Lord would appoint the singers and musicians to lead the armies of Israel into battle (2 Chron. 20:21). The ark was transported to Jerusalem with a fanfare of music (1 Chron. 15). David appointed music and song before the ark to host night and day prayer and worship for 33 years (1 Chron. 16:4). Just as the book of Psalms shows us, prayer and praise was designed to go together. Revelation 5:8 tells us that heaven uses harp (music) and bowl (prayers) in their perpetual worship service.

Singing your prayers is a great way to stay engaged in your time and a primary way to strengthen yourself in the Lord. David (the man after God's own heart) was a musician and built a massive community of musicians and singers, complementing day and night prayer. I think we should value music!

III. PRAY IN THE SPIRIT

One of the reasons people don't adopt a prayer life is because they feel they have to pray in their understanding and verbalize in their minds the whole time. Although I think praying in our understanding is important, there is a prayer language that will help us connect with God, especially when we know not how to pray.

I'm not gonna elaborate here because I've devoted a whole chapter to the truth of praying in the Spirit in chapter six.

IV. PRAY THE WORD

Much like praying in the Spirit, this is one way to know that we are praying the will of God. Applying Scripture to our prayer times gives us confidence that we are aligning our hearts and minds with the sure will of God. Faith (which comes by hearing the word) is heightened when we pray the word (Romans 10:17). It's the prayer of faith that carries breakthrough power (James 5:15).

Praying the Psalms and Apostolic Prayers (prayers that the apostles prayed) will help you stay engaged with the heart of God. There are thousands of passages to swim in, and they invite us into deeper encounter with God.

V. TAKE YOUR TIME AND SLOW DOWN

We live in a culture where most everything is running at very high speeds. This can often bleed over into our prayer time, where we feel that have to "run through" our prayer lists. Rushing through our devotion times with nervous anxiety, robs us of hearing God in the still small voice - the voice that shapes prophets and hearing people like it did Elijah.

I personally like to set aside at least one hour when I pray. Most of the time, it will take 15-20 minutes just to get focused and engaged.

If you are ever going to practice a life of prayer, you must understand that it's not all about speaking many words. Prayer is mostly about cultivating intimacy with Jesus. Though words are an avenue of prayer, there are times where things are quiet and void of words, yet we are still connecting with Him. Many of my greatest times in prayer have been when I said very little.

A LETTER FROM THE AUTHOR

Whether you have been praying for years or have just decided to embrace a lifestyle of prayer, I am excited about your journey. And more importantly, heaven and it's hosts are even more excited. I want to encourage you to lean on the Lord's faithfulness. As we've discussed, prayer takes on many forms and includes various emotions and dynamics. However, I encourage you to yield a simple "YES" to the Lord. Go ahead and ask Him for grace for the journey. Ask that He would strengthen you with divine perspective to remain faithful and fruitful in this journey of prayer. He wants to bless you more than you can even imagine. He's a good Father!

On the other end of this book, is a generation of saints longing for the deep things of God. So, understand that you're in good company. You are not alone. You are joining a multitude of believers who are shaping history by the ministry of prayer and intercession. What a joy this is to partner with Him.

I bless you in your journey. Along with other saints across the globe, I am praying for you. I am asking that God would infuse you with power and strengthen you in the inner man. I'm asking that He would open your eyes to see yourself before the throne with the hosts of heaven, declaring the holiness and worth of God. You are part of that great concert and crescendo of prayer in this generation! Beloved, you have a voice in this journey and I pray that you would continue to grow in the grace and peace of our Lord Jesus. Full speed ahead!

Blessings!